# VICTORY IN THE VALLEYS

# Victory

## IN THE VALLEYS

### THE GRIT REQUIRED TO BE MADE FOR MORE

NATALIE MCCOY

LANGLEY COLLECTIVE, LLC - TEXAS

First Edition

Publisher: Self-Published

ISBN: 979-8-9935875-0-9

A Note from the Author:

This book reflects my experiences, thoughts, and lessons learned the hard way. While it is meant to inform, inspire, and connect, it is not a substitute for professional advice. I hope it encourages readers to find strength, perspective, and courage in their own journeys.

Printed in the United States

This book is dedicated to my husband and my daughters. Y'all are my world, my reason for writing this story, and my reason to fight fearlessly regardless of my adversary.

I love you agape.

"Fear not, for I am with you;
be not dismayed, for I am your God;
I will strengthen you, I will help you,
I will uphold you with my
righteous right hand."

—Isaiah 41:10

# CONTENTS

# FOREWORD

When I think of Natalie—"Nat"—the first word that comes to mind is strength. Not the loud, spotlight kind, but the quiet, steady, grace filled strength that only comes from walking through fire and still choosing faith. As her best friend, I've had the privilege of watching her live out the words in this memoir long before they were ever written on a page.

This book isn't theory. It's testimony.

Nat has carried roles that come with both honor and hardship, standing steadfast through deployments as a military spouse, fighting through the unthinkable as a cancer patient, and emerging with the hard won strength of a survivor. Each of those seasons could have broken her spirit. Instead she allowed them to deepen her hope, sharpen her purpose, and anchor her more firmly in the God who never left her side. What you will read here is not just a story of hardship, it is a story of how faith shows up in the unknown, how love holds steady in waiting, and how courage looks in real life.

This memoir is both deeply personal and beautifully practical. Nat doesn't share her journey; she invites you into it. She speaks to the military spouse trying to stay strong across distance and deployment, to the cancer patient staring down a diagnosis they never asked for, to the survivor learning how to live again, and to the believer wondering where God is when the world starts coming apart. Her words carry the kind of honesty that makes you exhale and the kind of faith that makes you believe again.

Whether you are in the middle of your own battle or walking alongside someone who is, this book will meet you where you are. You'll find inspiration that lifts, wisdom that applies to real life, and reminders that even in the deepest valleys, God is present, able, and faithful.

As you turn these pages, I pray you'll see what I've seen in Nat for years, that hope is not fragile, faith is not theoretical, and survival is not the end of the story. There is beauty in what she lived, and there is purpose in what she now shares. I'm honored to stand beside her, and I'm grateful that you now get to walk with her too. And considering we've been navigating life together since college (a.k.a. the Nat & V Show) and she's the one who introduced me to my husband, Chad.

I feel especially qualified to say this: if she tries to downplay how incredible this book is, ignore her. I've earned lifetime bragging rights and at least partial credit for being her unpaid hype woman.

*—Dr. Vanessa "V" Smith*

# INTRODUCTION

I'm a kid born in the 80s and raised in the 90s so I think I got the best of both lives. I grew up in a world without cell phones and internet driving all the conversations; decisions and overall input that we get nowadays. I grew up in a time that I miss. I miss who we all were when we could sit down and talk face to face and that was the preferred method of communication. My childhood was full of simpler times, more activity and adventure and I'm so grateful for parents that made that happen for me.

I miss who we all were before September 11, 2001, and I miss who we became on September 12, 2001. I hope that we can return to being a country that stands together without having to experience a tragedy like 9/11 to get us there. We are the great United States of America, and all that love is down in there deep somewhere; we just need to get it out and use it to serve one another well. September 11th, while not discussed in this book, played a major role in my life and it shaped what my adult life looks like including my disdain for flying. I'm working on it. I'm a work in progress. That day would create the path that led my husband into my life, because it was part of his journey too. It's part of the reason he joined the military, and as time passes his generational era of Airmen are fading towards retirement and starting their new careers as civilians. They are the era that went to war. They saw and lived the things most Americans would never want to do or see. My husband did them, he was there and so were his friends. This generation of active-duty members have an immense amount of experience in the world and its cultures and life in general. People don't talk to them about it enough. They are a treasure trove of stories and information, as were each of the wartime generations before them. September 11 will forever be deeply ingrained into us and our families. You'll see that I, at times, have a tone and stance you may not like or agree with but that's my view and it's okay if you don't agree.

This book serves as a way for me to share my experiences, while dolling out lessons I've learned but it also an opportunity to give purpose to my life. As career military folks move toward retirement many  began to panic inside because they are moving into a new phase of life- the unknown. They've spent 20+ years excelling in the military and then one day they wake up civilian. There's a mourning process that goes with that feeling of loss. It's time to start anew except you're in your forties. Not only will this become my own reality at home, but I also spent many hours as part of my job helping navigate purpose and how to find it for the men and women I have served. It can be painful to work through this and honestly, it was painful for me to watch. I hated watching them feel like they were losing themselves. My husband will be no different, but we will get there, together.

You'll see that cancer creates those same feelings and challenges. I've been searching since diagnosis to find what my updated purpose on this earth will be. I've always known that it had to include sharing the love of Jesus, but I haven't done well at executing that. Writing this book is part of that purpose. I got enough comments on social media, messages, texts, and face to face comments about how I should write a book and share my story—so here we are. This is now a piece of my purpose and I'm hoping that somewhere here you find something that helps you, motivates you, or makes something click for you.

I am a Christian and a sinner. I am forgiven. I am the wife of an enlisted military member. I am a cancer survivor. I am a mom. I am a friend. I am a caregiver. I'm passionate about doing things that I feel have purpose and doing them right. Dreams are only crazy if there's no work ethic behind them. I write exactly how I talk so this book should be taken as a casual conversation with lots of ups and downs. If I tried to do this any other way, it would be terrible. It's just who I am and what I am not, is professional writer.

As a 90s kid, I loved me some Magic School Bus, so that's how I saw this book play out in my head. It's one journey at a time with brief points of returning to normalcy.

So, come with me on a field trip! Seatbelts y'all, cause this trip may get wild!

As the fantastic Ms. Frizzle once said,

"To the bus!"

# 1

## ADULTING IS WILD: MY VIEW AS AN ENLISTED AIR FORCE WIFE

A born and raised Texan, I grew up thinking I would do what "most good southern girls do: college, grad school, married." I'd then find some Wrangler wearing Texas boy, we'd date for a while, be engaged for a year, and then get married. We'd live there in Texas, never moving too far from our mama's— a nice, safe, steady life. The problem here is I'm not built that way. Call me a color outside the lines kinda girl. I've been that way as long as I can remember. It made me a lot to handle, too much for some people and not enough of "the right stuff" for others, but that's who I am. It helped make me successful in my career, and it has served me well as an adult. In that spirit, I should give you a spoiler alert: the plan went a bit rogue.

Middle and high school were a little weird, but you go find me someone who just adored those years and says they were "normal." Education was important to me, so I followed those college then graduate school steps "correctly." I graduated high school a year early (on a whim), went straight to college then straight to graduate school. I feel like I get bonus points for that. When choosing a graduate school, I had a moment of uncertainty where I changed my acceptance from one school to another after I had already accepted the first. I felt deep down in my gut that I was supposed to be at the school I ultimately chose, even though it paid me slightly less and I would have to teach. I didn't want to teach, and I didn't want to be paid less, but I couldn't shy away from my gut telling me to switch. I felt so bad when I withdrew my first acceptance to make the switch, but something told me that it would change my life. As I finished grad school, I met this incredible guy that turned my life plan on its head. Thank you, gut feeling, for leading me to the right school! He was a young airman whom I had known from working on the base at the gym. We had been gym acquaintances for a year or so, but never really had a conversation. If I'm being honest, I never paid attention to how good looking he was, because he didn't fit that mold of "good 'ol Texas boy." He was a Chuck Taylor wearing bald guy with tattoos. One invitation from him to hang out and watch a movie with his friends led to a date, which turned into a relationship. On that first date I had a gut feeling that I couldn't ignore, and it was telling me that I would marry him. I knew most of my friends would think I was crazy, so I only told my roommate and my best friend from college.

Three months into dating he was tasked for his first deployment. It was 2009 and we were still very much at war in the Middle East. II knew that dating him came with challenges, deployments, and—in his career field—shift work, but I hadn't expected the deployments to come so soon. Four months into dating, he deployed. Looking back now, we laugh about him preparing to leave. We never really discussed whether we were staying together or breaking up. We made zero plans or decisions. We just continued like nothing was happening (like standing in a dumpster fire, smiling and drinking coffee). I think we both just assumed we were staying together. The night before his departure, he told me he thought he loved me. Reciprocating that sentiment was easy because I already knew deep down that he was it for me, but I had to be cool about it; I didn't want to seem needy. I said, "I feel the same." Cool, I know.

The next morning, we all gathered at the airport for the big "see you later". He was on a team of about thirteen and everyone's family and friends were there; squadron leadership and members were there too. This was a regional airport y'all. It wasn't built to be that packed. I'll never forget looking around and taking that all in. It was overwhelming, the patriotism was palpable in the room; from the team, from us, and from all the civilians also just trying to get to their flight. People stopped to talk to the team, people prayed for them, said good luck to them, and thanked them. It was my very first "see you later." PDA (public displays of affection) aren't allowed in uniform so each team member stood and hugged their loved ones as hard as they could, maybe snuck a quick kiss, and walked away to board the plane. I remember seeing guys kneeling on the floor hugging their crying kids and I had to fight back a tear. It was hard to watch them walk away and board. I had no idea what I was getting into.

The deployment ended up being about nine months. The longest nine months full of anxiety, from waiting for phone calls and emails, to not knowing how he was doing and watching the news about the region I knew he was in. It was a steep learning curve.

You see; there's no preparation, instruction manual, or class on how to be with someone in the military. If there was it would change all the time and have 1,947 editions. Learning to live this lifestyle means rising to the occasion and being adaptable at a high rate of speed. It's a special breed of people that take on the challenge of living the way we live. Military families can become isolated very easily. I've been told several times in several different states when meeting people that, "we don't become friends with military people because you just leave." That is one of the hardest sentences I've ever had to digest. Sometimes we only identify with each other. It can be very challenging for introverts, but it always brings people together. This is a shared experience that doesn't compare to anything else. It can be the hardest thing you've ever done and the most rewarding thing you'll ever do, all on a Monday.

Communication during deployments is never easy, but especially fifteen plus years ago. Keep in mind; this first deployment was in 2009. We were at war and video calls weren't really a thing then. I come from the era where the internet and cell phones didn't exist when I was born, and came into existence in my youth; make of that what you will. From Iraq, I would receive a thirteen minute-ish phone call every five to ten days that he had to stand in a forty-five minute or more line for, and between that and email, that's how we communicated. There were plenty of times one of us would be connected to the wrong person by the base operator, and we'd end up talking to someone else's grandpa or girlfriend —annoying, yet entertaining. I remember him emailing one time to say that the operator connected him to someone's grandpa that didn't understand that my boyfriend was NOT his grandson. So rather than end the call he just talked to the old guy so that he could sleep that night thinking he'd talked to his grandson.

One month had passed in his first deployment, with an unknown number of months still to go. Then he called me with a serious conversation.

This day and call were different. He had a serious tone, and I got nervous. He said, "I think we should get married sooner than we talked about." I was in shock. I knew I had thought it, and I knew it was what I wanted, but I didn't know he had felt the same. Knowing we were on a timer, we rapidly talked through a couple things. I needed to make sure that I understood what was happening. Was he asking me to marry him?! On the phone?! From Iraq?! Come to think of it, I didn't remember us ever talking about it so I said, "Are you talking about like this calendar year soon, or in the next five years soon?" to which he replied, "I mean when I get home." I told him my dad HAD to be involved. Good southern girl, remember? Turns out, that part was taken care of via email. He said he used email to talk with my dad so one of my phone calls wouldn't be used. I was impressed. That's real planning and thoughtfulness—this wasn't a whim for him. I knew then he was going to be my greatest adventure. I said, "Yes, let's do this!" There I was, engaged, no ring, no video of a proposal, no guy on one knee in front of all my friends—just a thirteen minute conversation from another country that changed my life forever.

Deployment #1 was taking forever. He wanted to get married right after he returned home, so I was to spend the remainder of the deployment planning a wedding. It was a great way to burn up time. I can't say how many people thought I was crazy, but I'm confident it was in the hundreds. In every bridal shop I drew all kinds of looks, because there I was; no ring, no bridesmaids, and no plan. I was whole-heartedly ready to marry a guy I'd dated for four months before he left the country for nine more.

The final thirty days felt like sixty days and their return home date changed at least five times with only twenty-four hours' notice. The roller coaster of returning home is something I'll never enjoy. It's like being five years old and someone hands you an ice cream cone, then right as you lean in for that first lick, they snatch it from your hand and say, "Oops! Sorry, that one was for your brother. I'll get you one tomorrow." Expect the return-home process to mean that you'll have that cone snatched several times—maddening.

Think about movies where the main character is bee-bopping down the street after something fantastic has happened to them. The sun is bright, outfit is on point, hair is perfect, coffee in hand, and it doesn't matter that a street fight is taking place on the corner. All is right in the world. That's how I would describe homecomings. I could care less about anything on that day—because on homecoming day, my family is whole again. I can hit the play button on life once more.

The first ever homecoming day was quite an experience. There we were, packed into the small airport again, nervous energy consuming everyone. It had been a rough nine months with many delays and hurdles, but we had finally made it. This time it felt like excitement instead of sadness. People from his squadron plus family and friends filled the whole waiting area. Seeing him walk off the plane was like fresh air filling my lungs. It meant my adult life was beginning, and I would soon be getting married!

Our wedding was everything I'd ever wanted but didn't know I needed. The day was beautiful, and the celebration was so much fun. Lots of friends and family came to celebrate with us. My husband has a large family, and I was shocked at how many of them made the trip to Texas for our wedding. It was amazing.

We had survived our first deployment and were married. We moved into our first little home together and settled into how to navigate our new life as a couple. We were shift workers on opposite shifts with one car. I went to work at 0415 to open the gym, and he worked nights. Nevertheless, we pushed forward—my husband promoted, we had friends, and we were enjoying being young and in the military. I knew that he loved kids and wanted at least two or three, but I wasn't ready. He was more prepared than me for sure. We decided to just be married for a few years before we added a kid to the mix. It would give us the chance to know each other well, have fun as a couple first and live some life before we had to take care of another human.

Deployment #2 came and went with a few good things and a plethora of problems. This one was also to Iraq, but a different location. It had its own learning curve, its own attacks, provided him a different mission than the first deployment, but the same difficulties related to communication. Missing home was different for him this time. This time we were married. I had the same concerns, but now it felt heavier. If something happened to him it was my husband I would lose. I won't go in depth on this tour, but he eventually returned home to the same airport as the first and the home-coming felt the same way! I just skipped my way on a sunny day right through all the world's BS taking place around me, and picked him up at the airport.

We were still stationed in Texas and close to my family, so I had it pretty good! After a few years we found out we were pregnant! It was so exciting, and our families were thrilled. Mine, in particular was overjoyed because they lived so close to us. Just as that venture began, he called me at work with another serious conversation. We had PCS (permanent change of station) orders. We were moving to Colorado, and we were leaving in ninety days. I would be five and a half months pregnant when we arrived in Colorado and the pressure was on to get appointments on top of normal PCS burdens. If you've ever watched 90s kid TV you're familiar with how I felt when I sing," Now this is a story all about how my life got flipped upside down." Nevertheless, it was exciting. I loved Colorado, had traveled there annually for much of my life to ski, and had always wanted to live there. We bought our first home, packed everything up, and off we went into the wild blue yonder (Lil Air Force shout-out there).

Our first daughter was born just a couple months after we arrived, and the world seemed complete. Our families were great about coming to visit us, and that support has lasted our entire military career. It's something I know I'm lucky to have. Some people join the military to get away from their families and go out and build their own. It's good for that too. The military will break you down in many ways, but it is the ultimate teacher. You learn more about yourself, the world, and how to work with others from all over the world than you ever could staying in one place your whole life. I learned over the years that just when we think we've made it and we've got it covered, God shows us his sense of humor.

Deployment #3 was in the works and this time it would be Afghanistan. Afghanistan won't get much coverage from me here. It was hard. That's all you need to know. We had a baby, I had just returned to work, and he was leaving again. Deployments are just part of life, and I knew that. I was never angry or distraught about them as irritating as they can be. They were necessary and I knew he was serving with purpose and that was good enough for me. He missed so much over the years because of deployments and shift work, but resilience and durability are some of my strongest personality traits. Having a baby makes a deployment go by faster, I found because I was non-stop busy. This is the deployment where I discovered coffee! Hard to believe maybe, but I had never been a coffee drinker. I didn't know much about it honestly other than I liked the smell. Turns out I also like caffeine. Still in Colorado we loved the mountains, the camping, the hiking, the lakes, and the outdoor escapades.

About three years after our first daughter was born, our second daughter joined us. This was when my husband decided that weddings were expensive and we kept having girls. He said, "maybe we should stop at two kids before I can't afford all these weddings." He had a solid point. He was made to be a girl dad though. These two girls have him wrapped up like a professionally done ribbon-bow on an expensive Christmas package. You know, the kind you can't get off and it's too pretty to cut through?

Anyway, the first daughter was a preemie at about four weeks early but the obstacle ahead with our second daughter was an aggressive one. Our first had done well, she was growing, learning and she was amazing. She had overcome that premature birth like it was no big deal.

The second baby was seven weeks premature, landing us in the NICU for about twenty-five days followed by six months of an oxygen tank that we called "the ball and chain." I'll spare you the details of her birth story, but the short version was a bumpy road. The hospital I'd had my first daughter at was on base but when I showed up there, they immediately transferred me to a large hospital downtown. My vitals were sporadic; I was in and out of consciousness and it got scary. My blood pressure and breathing were tanking. I came to at the moment a doctor and nurse were running in to get me to an OR for a c-section so they could stabilize me and the baby. As soon as I awoke it became clear (to me anyway) that I wouldn't make it to an OR. This kid was coming. I said, "Nope. We're doing this right now! This baby is ready." And she was. Instead of a c-section, she made her appearance right then and was rushed to the NICU. By the time I got to see her several hours later, my mom had landed in Colorado, gone to the NICU and helped give her a bath. To be fair, my mom didn't know that I hadn't gotten to see her, and I don't know that she knew how dire my medical situation had become. In true grandma fashion she had been able to see my kid before me, and she got that baby bathed and in her NICU bed.

Both our girls are now healthy and strong, praise God! I know many military wives have gone through the same, but many went through them while their husband was deployed. Finding support in your military family is so powerful and so accessible. We all make friends fast, love them hard and show up when they need it because we never know how long we have together, so we have to make it count.

Our time in Colorado was rewarding. We grew professionally, as parents, as a couple and individually. We had a great church there that had been a blessing to our lives and brought us both back closer to where we should be spiritually. We grew immensely as a family in that church.

We had cruised through the first eight-ish years of marriage and had accomplished so much including building our family that was now a four-pack of fun.

# 2

## INDEPENDENCE SPARKS GROWTH

Over the course of this book there will be truths and lessons learned woven in. Being independent becomes a necessity when your husband is deployed and you have to get things done. The "things" aren't going to do themselves, so every spouse has to dig out that special, sparkly pair of big girl undies and saddle up. When they leave, the world falls apart like clockwork, without fail—Murphy's Law (you know, the one about things going wrong, and deployments are one and the same), I think. Independence and learning to do tasks you don't want to do can be incredibly freeing and will become celebrated over the years as you become acclimated and mature in your spouse role.

Spouses (all y'all, not just military, but especially military)—have your own tool bag and know how to use the tools in it. Learn to fix household things: loose doorknobs, running toilets, leaky faucets, broken kids' toys, dead batteries, broken cabinets, and unbuilt furniture are simple and you are capable. You don't NEED your husband to fix those things. It's cool to want him to, and allow him to do it once he returns, but you're a whole adult and you can do it. You just need a little dedication, knowledge and maybe some online videos to figure it out. Regardless, don't let a door or faucet be what takes you down. You're better than that and smart enough to overcome. College education can be helpful, but street smarts and ingenuity win the day during deployments. Expectations of uneventful and smooth deployments are just premeditated resentments; don't get caught in that.

If you've never had to do your wills before a deployment in your twenties these things may seem silly, but they aren't. The risk was and is real. Writing your will is a gut check and brings perspective to a situation you never knew you'd be in. They are usually re-done with each deployment, and they are easier to do as you gain experience, but the first one is a shock to the soul. It forces you to focus and reflect and instantly you are more mature than when you walked into the room. There are key things that should be done before departure because they may be easily forgotten once you enter the overwhelming couple of weeks just before they leave. I've come across some spouses that were truly helpless for various reasons, but don't let that reason be lack of preparation.

I've always spent time with the youngest wives making sure they understood the weight of the situation: that they had what they needed, knew how to navigate communication, got resources, and had some things planned while their husband was gone. Have a hobby or get one. Overall, learning to be independent, thinking for yourself and acting quickly on your feet are critical to successfully surviving military life, not just deployments. Living a life of dependence on your spouse doesn't bode well. I learned to do so many unplanned things because the military demanded that I figure it out on my own and I'm thankful for the forced proficiency. I did a lot of growing up, maturing and becoming who I am because of hard situations.

Planning so in-depth feels like overkill, but it's not—so do it anyway. It's the one time you should consider all the "what-ifs" in life. You might think to yourself, "Gina Marie, you're doing too much. You're being extra—just chill." But don't chill cause you're not extra….you're exact and I promise you'll be happy you did it. Get Ready, Be Ready and Stay Ready. Don't get in a pickle because you did a crappy prep job.

Case and Point: During deployment #3 I got a little cocky. I mean, it was #3 on top of numerous TDYs (temporary duty assignment), exercises that were local, my own TDYs and two kids. I GOT THIS. I have to say… I was a deployed spouse veteran by now. I knew having knee surgery during a deployment would be a hot mess, but there aren't many dumpster fires at this point that I don't pull up to and just get out with my s'mores bucket. It's fine.

And really, it was OK, but the problem was I didn't prepare for myself. Turns out when I'm unchecked and on pain meds I really LIKE ONLINE SHOPPING. Now, I've had many surgeries at this point and this one was minor, so I didn't need another adult after the first twenty-four hours. I was partially mobile and could manage myself with crutches just fine. A friend took me to surgery and back home. No big deal....until I was left alone with my wallet in reach. (Since this, I've just memorized my card numbers so now I have real reckless potential!) I have a thing for wreaths—got me three of them from right there on the couch. Didn't even know I'd bought them until I started getting shipping notifications a couple of weeks later and I had to dig through my purchase history. I called my mom at 0200 convinced I needed a pressure cooker after watching an infomercial. She talked me out of that one, thankfully. At some point in the 48-hour post-surgery timeframe I texted a friend that lived two streets over and told her I needed some help. Apparently, I didn't clarify the "with what" part and when she got to my house the doors were locked. So, in natural military spouse fashion, she found herself an open window and barrel rolled into my house only to hear me say, "thank goodness you're here. That light is blasting me in the eyes, and I haven't slept all night because of it. Can you just turn it off?" I would have round house kicked me if I had showed up and come through a window for that.... but she politely turned it off, filled up my water and left through the door.

We all learn quickly how to jump in and help each other in times of our spouse's absence. You become willing to help people in situations you would have never previously allowed yourself to be a part of because there aren't other options. We have each other. Being a military spouse is an action-packed existence, it's a lifestyle, it has its own personality, and it creates a spirit of grit, pride, self-confidence and independence that I personally have never felt anywhere else. We are a different breed of people, and I lean into that.

It's not an insult. It's an honor.

This life is not for everybody and there are those that struggle. The job the rest of us have in that instance is to support those who struggle, bring them out of their shell, and immerse them in community. We are a small percentage of the population, and our milestones, hurdles, and struggles aren't relatable to others in many circumstances. We are continuously searching for jobs even though many of us are trained, certified and licensed in long-term career fields, every time we move, we learn a new school system on top of how our new state or country has their education system set up. Our kids may be in advanced classes in one state, and our new school may be significantly behind when we arrive. Sometimes our spouses leave, and we are worried about their safety, worried about the unknown of when we'll hear from them, and worried about how we'll explain to our kids that their parent has been injured. The worst thought of all: worried that the day may come where we're forced to tell our kids that their parent was killed. That's not normal, it's not how most of America functions, but it's how we function.

You may think my thoughts are dark and off the mark, but I don't give advice on things I have not experienced myself. You may say that I'm being dramatic…I've been called dramatic—among many other things.

Read that again.

Someone told me that I WAS BEING DRAMATIC when I voiced my worries about my husband who I hadn't heard from in days while he sat in a war zone. Wrong choice, ma'am. On top of that, I couldn't talk about those worries when I was at home because my kids were there and I wouldn't dare scare them with something like that. It was the entire reason I'd voiced my worries to another adult.

This is the kind of independence during a deployment that just sucks. Dealing with your own emotions, the kid's emotions, and an outsider's lack of emotional intelligence is exhausting. If you're not a military spouse but are friends with one, try to have grace. They may be going through something they won't tell you about because it won't make sense to you or it's too much to explain, but they still need you as a friend.

Words matter. There are plenty of "helpful" phrases or comparisons people like to throw out in an effort to make you feel better, but they don't.

~~I don't need you to offload how bad your day was because your husband was late coming home, your kids acted up, everyone was late to practice, and you have no dinner plan. Because you know what? SAME, but I'm also concerned for my husband's safety while dealing with identical problems on my own.~~

OK, now that I've matured, I see that anger response as unnecessary and destructive.

When supporting us, try not to use fluff and catchy phrases like: "it's only a few more months," or, "I'm sure he's fine, you're just overthinking it" or "well you know God won't give you more than you can bear," (which is my least favorite of all and not true). We don't need that, and we don't want it. We need you to show up and maybe just sit in silence with us, or drink coffee and chit-chat. We need you to accept that we just need to worry and be sad and maybe mad for a few minutes and that's OK. We don't need a bunch of words to fix us or make it better—because you can't.

So, friends—military and non—a spouse going on a work trip for a week, while I know it is irritating and disruptive to your life, is not the same as a deployment. I know non-military spouses are just trying to relate and show understanding, but it can make things worse. It's important to know that I do care about life happenings that go on with all my friends. I like to talk to others about what's going on with them, hear how their day was, and hear what they're struggling with.

We need local spouse friends. We need your friendship and your perspective on life. We like your stability and how you go about your life with family near you. We truly love that you adopted us into your local friend tribe when it would have been easier for you to just move past us. We really do appreciate and need you!

So, what do we do when it all becomes too much? We call in another military spouse, we pour a glass of wine or coffee, we talk, we vent, sometimes we cry and then…we press.

# THE REMOTE TOUR

# 3

## IF IT WAS EASY, EVERYONE WOULD DO IT

We had lived in Colorado for six years, thriving, growing our family, learning to grow into a church family, and working with some amazing people, but we both felt stagnant. We knew we were made to do more than we were doing in Colorado. Six years is a long time to be in one place, so my husband began to look for what was next.

He, per the usual, called me one day at work and said, "I have an opportunity to do a remote tour. I have to get it out of the way at some point and if I'm going to be gone for a whole year, I want it to really mean something. How do you feel about me going to BLEEEEP for a year?" (Sorry, I can't give away all locations but just know that it wasn't a normal remote tour.) A remote tour means you are leaving without your family for at least a year. These are locations where families don't go or aren't allowed to go. It's expected in most career fields that at some point (if you want to promote) you do a remote tour.

His first deployment was so long that it had originally met the criteria, but that criteria had changed and it no longer qualified. He wanted to do something that majority of the Air Force would never get to do, he wanted it to matter, and he wanted it to have purpose. All these things led us away from the standard remote and this new opportunity existed in an extraordinary location and would be a once-in-a-lifetime operational accomplishment. Few people bagged the chance to do this assignment because the team is so small, there were a lot of criteria the candidate had to meet for eligibility, and they were selective in who they brought to the team. I understood the uniqueness of the mission and how impactful it could be, but it was a lot to take over one phone call. He said, "I have to let them know pretty quickly. Like, by tomorrow... and today would be ideal, but I know this is a lot. Think about it and I'll come over and talk to you in person shortly." I've almost always worked on base so it made hard conversations like this easier because we could just quickly meet to discuss things. I went back and forth when we hung up about the pros and cons, the impact on our kids, the three to four months of trainings and TDYs (temporary duty assignments) that would take place prior to this year even beginning and deciding if I could handle it all. Our kids were younger, which led me to believe that if we needed to do a remote at some point we might as well do it while they were younger and wouldn't have as detailed a memory of it versus having preteens and teens to deal with on my own—no thank you!

By the time he arrived in my office, I'd decided that he should do it. My gut was nudging me to support him and know we would be fine. He accepted the offer and immediately they began sending him training instructions, reporting instructions and information. We were off to the races, and it was fast. This location required an immense amount of preparation and training. He would essentially be on his own. He would live on a base, but not one that was American. He wouldn't have access to medical; finance or personnelists and he would only have four other Americans with him as part of this team. There would be a mountain of information and cultural education to climb through, and this assignment would be the biggest challenge he'd faced—and he would face it solo. I held fear for him but tried to keep it to myself, he was stressed trying to get all the training complete and arrive on time. We had to complete preparations with about four months until he was supposed to arrive in country. The training would take three months so the amount of time we had together prior to him leaving shrunk significantly once the ball started rolling. This would become the hardest separation we would experience. There were so many obstacles, two valleys for every mountain we climbed, and I ended up taking care of almost everything related to home on my own prior to departure. We operated in silos for the time leading up to him leaving simply to accomplish everything on time.

Some said I was crazy to agree to this tour. I'm not crazy, I just have intimate understanding of how the military works and what it takes to make that career successful. My husband and I make decisions as a team. He didn't agree to that assignment and THEN call me to tell me. He called me first; it was a discussion (albeit quick) and then he accepted the assignment. We knew that we could handle that assignment as a family, and he knew I could handle it as his wife. Some people are not up for that kind of thing and that's OK. There's more than one way to have career success in the military, but for his path and career field this was the road we needed to take, and we chose that road *together*.

My intuition hasn't steered me wrong yet, so I knew this was right. Once this year away was complete, we would have orders, and it would be on to the new chapter in our story. In growing spiritually, I acknowledged my gut feelings as Holy Spirit-driven, with the intent to guide me, but they were to be prayed over with discernment.

Location aside, this was another region of the Middle East that we didn't really have an American presence, and it presented its own challenges and opportunities. I would watch the news, like I did for the prior deployments to Iraq and Afghanistan, so I could get a feel for the war climate from week to week. My usual morning thoughts were:

Were things going well there?

Were people being attacked regularly or at all?

Were there any reports of injured Americans that day?

I had so many concerns, and what I found was—his region was rarely, if ever, covered in mainstream media. I had to go search for the information sources myself. It was a weird time to live in. I could turn on a TV, search websites, or go old school, find a newspaper, and instantly know tons of things about world events. Except for now, when I really needed it. I couldn't find anything without really searching.

Explaining to people where he was and what he was doing, I kept vague, and it felt sneaky not to tell family and friends, but it needed to be that way. I felt like I was making up a story every time I talked about it, and I was sure people thought I was exaggerating, dramatizing, and overselling this story. But I wasn't and nobody could relate. I no longer had a circle of deployment buddies paying attention to the same region I was. I was a lone wolf instead of deep into a wolf pack this time. Nobody else knew what was happening there, so every time something suspect took place, I was on my own. There was a point in the year where the country he was in and the neighboring country began escalating tensions and then slowly began acting on it. My husband and his small team were stuck, far from other Americans, hours away from help and things were heating up. While I can't give you all the details of that event, I will tell you it was the most stressful forty-eight hours I experienced of the whole tour. I can't imagine how he felt!

He called me and said, "Hey, babe. It's really bad over here. I have a lot of things to accomplish to make sure we have accountability for everyone. I don't know when I'll be able to call you again but it's going to be a few days. Watch BEEEEP news station for updates and that should give you an idea of how it's going. Love you, I'll contact you when I can. Gotta go."

And that was it.

I was on my own to wonder, wait, hope, and pray that they would all be OK. Again, I tried to find someone to talk to, but I couldn't. He was off their radar because he wasn't technically deployed; he had PCS'd to this remote location. The base that serviced any of his needs was in another state. I talked to them regularly for assistance correcting documents, but it wasn't like there was a support system to which I could just call and vent. After several days, I made the decision that his commander at the squadron he'd left needed to know the situation. I thought, maybe, the commander would have a channel to get information about his status before I could. At a minimum, his commander cared about his people, and I was still there and volunteering in the squadron. I was still "his people," and I was in dire need of communication. I met with him and gave the rundown of events. I felt more validated afterwards because he had genuine concern, like I did. He went to work looping in people so that they could track the situation.

Here I was again, trying to do it all on my own because I'm self-sufficient. Remember, I can handle all the things, but I couldn't handle this. I didn't have the resources to get information or people to relate to my stress. I had finally taken the step I needed to and reached out for help. I wasn't sure he'd be able to find anything out, but it felt so good to get it all out to someone who understood and could verify that my concerns weren't dramatic or crazy. I needed to know that I wasn't just being extra about it all!

Ultimately, the commander was able to gather some intel and told me what I was allowed to know. That's plenty good for me. I know I can't know all those details, but knowing that they could verify the situation and that he was OK was enough. The commander understood the seriousness of the situation and continued to check in with me until I heard from him.

A day or two more came and went, and then my phone pinged; it was an email. The email was short, but it was always his way of sending me proof of life. It just said, "Check BEEEEP news station. Read the article that posted this morning. I'm OK. Love you." The overwhelming relief that came with that email is indescribable. In an instant, my blood pressure dropped, the knot in my stomach started to relax, and my nausea began to subside. Through every deployment there had been plenty of times that we would lose communication as soon as an attack kicked off or he was called in for an emergency or fifty other reasons. I sat through so many video calls where we had to pause seven or eight times per call because he lived right by a flight line and all I could hear were planes taking off. The times that comms went out were the hardest because you never know when they'll be up and running again. But this guy of mine is good. Even if he was busy and his life was crazy there, as soon as he could I'd get a quick proof of life email. They usually only consisted of two phrases:

"I'm OK. Love you." That's enough for me.

My husband is a fighter, a survivor, the calm in the storm, and usually the quietest guy in the room. That's only because he's always formulating which plan he'll use if anything in that room goes sideways. He's the guy that everyone constantly asks, "You OK, man?" and he just has to respond, "Yeah, it's just my face." He's a deep thinker that has a plan with three back-up plans. He has always been a good communicator because he knows that I can process feelings better if I have all the details, good or bad. Even if he had died on one of those deployments I would want to know how and what happened because I could get through it more efficiently that way. I appreciate him for that. He gets me. I'm the only one who truly sees the real him. He could be deadly if the situation had required it, but he is mostly calm and collected. It takes a lot to get him wound up and that makes him steady, level-headed, and strong-willed. These are some of his greatest traits. He is made of gold in my eyes. These exceptional traits would take center stage later in our journey in ways we'd never considered.

That year tested my resolve in ways I couldn't fathom. My only alone time was when I showered each night after both kids were asleep. You'll see in a later chapter all the things I learned during deployments and this remote. I added a plethora of things to that list during the year.

On a remote tour you get to do a "mid-tour "trip home for fourteen days. That trip had become my source of motivation for the year. We chose to do his mid-tour slightly past the halfway point because it would leave us a "downhill side" that was shorter, and it also lined up better with his teammates trying to schedule their mid-tours. I spent countless hours planning this trip. I put a lot of thought and care into what it would consist of. People get so creative with mid-tours, so I had tons of ideas I'd seen from other spouses. We could simply just hang out at home as a family. We could take a mini-vacation somewhere close, we could go on a big trip like a cruise or major destination, but none of that felt right to me. Neither my husband nor I like or" do well" in large, crowded places. I didn't want to be confined to a cruise ship, and we would be bored in three days if we just sat at home. So, what was I going to do that wouldn't break the bank, but be fun? I didn't really want my kids to see him in their house because I knew they would think he was home for good. If they saw him back in the house the departure following this trip home would be even harder than the first one. I made the decision we had to be on vacation. Did it suck for him; probably. I didn't let him come home, but he understood why I was planning it that way. Point of fact, he only spent one night in our house during that mid tour, and it was to pack his vacation bag. We covered three states in fourteen days and decided this would be a trip to see our families (who we always have fun with), take our kids to do fun things, and we would stop through to the base we were going to be PCSing to and check it out! We already knew the next assignment was going to be Missouri, we just didn't have hard orders yet.

The trip was so fun. We went to Texas, did a resort (which mostly consisted of us being in a lazy river, at the pool, or by a firepit) and the kids loved it. We went to Missouri and saw my in-laws who happened to live just on the other side of the state from where we would be stationed. The kids got to see their cousins, and we went on a mini trip with them to smaller destinations in Missouri. We closed it out with a visit to our new base. The kids had a blast! Getting to see their new school before arrival is cool and doesn't happen very often. The planning and the trip were perfect. It was exactly what we needed to get ourselves through the remaining months of the tour.

The second round of departure came, and it was hard. It was hard to watch my girls hug their daddy and not want him to go. It was hard knowing that months still lie ahead of stress and worry. It was hard hugging him and knowing that would be it for a while. But it was exciting because it was the downhill side. We had arrived at the point where I could start a countdown. I had lots to do to prepare for us to move, and the planning for that kept me busy.

At one point, I got pneumonia after weeks of fighting bronchitis that wouldn't go away with medication. During that illness, the daycare on base called me to tell me both my kids had to be picked up because they had fevers. Both girls had the flu, and all three of us were miserable. Our families being twelve to fourteen hours away was rough when stuff like this came up. I needed to be in the hospital, but I couldn't with both girls sick and no family there. I barely left my couch for almost a week. I gathered all the strength I had and I made the girls a pallet of blankets and pillows on the floor beside me because I couldn't go up and down the stairs. I got out every can of soup we had and placed it on the counter along with bread and peanut butter and I filled their little unicorn water bottles up. I vividly remember that process wiping me out and wondering how we would get through it. My oldest daughter was five and the youngest was two. I led the oldest kid through how to heat up soup in the microwave from my spot on the couch. I heard her drag a barstool over to the microwave and with her sweet little voice she told me, "I got this mommy. I can take care of us." She knew how to make PB & J's so she was able to make sandwiches when I couldn't get up. She felt the least sick of the three of us and she's a true leader and helper with a sweet soul from Jesus. That week was so long and difficult, but we made it and added that to our list of things we learned to overcome.

I was learning to be more durable than before, and the growth was painful. Discomfort creates internal growth and growth propels us forward. I had to tell myself that diamonds are created under pressure, so I intended to come out of this assignment shiny and strong. It was a painful, long, stressful year. Lots of things went wrong at home, lots of things went wrong for him, but a new chapter of life was ahead!

Orders to the next base dropped before he was home. Colorado to Missouri! But you know by now that nothing great is easy in life, so naturally, our arrival date in Missouri was a month before his arrival home.

I was moving to Missouri on my own with two kids, a dog, and two vehicles. It wouldn't be a PCS if it were easy, friends! My grandpa used to tell me, "You can't ride two horses with one butt, kiddo." It was the first thing that came to mind when I realized I had two vehicles to move with my one butt. I had a lot of planning to do. Much more than a normal PCS. He was coming from overseas with a household goods shipment and I was moving stateside with the same.

Missouri is not where we asked to go. We asked to go to Alaska. I view Alaska like it's a frozen Texas with mountains. I had always wanted to go to Alaska, and this remote tour was supposed to have gotten us the orders we wanted—Alaska. The military rarely complies with what YOU want, even when you're supposed to get it. I had an enormous task ahead and time flew by as I prepared for our move. We decided to move ourselves like we had before because it would make us some money in the process, and who doesn't like to bulk up their savings when possible. Ohhhh, the list of tasks to accomplish seemed overwhelming. I needed to create continuity at work so the next person was set up for success, get the kids in school there and out of school in Colorado, move out of base housing, get a house in Missouri, transfer mail, get vehicles prepared, get a moving truck, schedule my parents to help me drive the truck, find time to pack and load everything amongst a thousand other things.

Military families know that we usually don't say goodbye to people. It's always, "see you later". See you later day finally came in Colorado. I like to think that we're all good at picking up right where we left off the next time we see each other. We're good at traveling to see friends we made along the way, and during that trip, if you're passing through a town where other friends live, you'll stop and see them too. We make family wherever we are, and some of them become lifelong friends that we travel near and far for. As we drove away, I was overcome with emotions. Seven very important years of my life were there, my kids were born there, and my husband wasn't even with me to drive away. I was staring at Pikes Peak, taking in the beauty of the mountain range, knowing it may be the last time I looked at that view. All of God's masterpiece was displayed straight ahead of me in a breathtaking mountain peak, the top covered in snow, golden and scarlet-leaved trees, and the sun shining.

Those emotions dried up as I turned at the first intersection, got on the interstate and headed into a new season of life.

# 4

## THE COLLECTION: LESSONS AND TRUTHS FROM AIR FORCE WIVES (OBTAINED THE HARD WAY)

This chapter contains all the things I, and a few other spouses I enlisted for input, have learned over the course of PCSs and deployments. It's obviously not all-inclusive, but it's random knowledge we've acquired. Spouses around the world could add to this list endlessly. Much of this list contains situations we've learned due to deployments, which made us single parents and the responsible party to address the mess (whatever it may be). It's truth, it's lessons and knowledge that seem ridiculously basic, but you didn't know it until now, because now you need it.

Military separations are incomparably experienced. Two spouses with deployed family members who are gone at the same time can have remarkably different events take place. This, in part, creates the adversity that must be overcome either during the deployment itself or upon return. Some people move home during deployment to be with their family; some stay. Some cry a lot; others not at all. Some feel sorry for themselves for months on end (the ones that really need a friend), and some act like nothing is happening. No matter how you deal with it...don't deal on your own. Find a friend. A deployment buddy. I have deployment buddies and cancer buddies you'll learn about later. We all need them whether we want them or not.

It's important to note that departure must be dealt with in whatever way works best for each family. Some spouses do not go inside the airport at all, and some go all the way to the gate; it's a deeply personal choice. I can't speak for them, but for me: I allow one pity party day. JUST ONE. When I leave the airport, and after I've told him to be safe, come home, and call me. I get in my truck, and I get it over with, if I'm going to cry. If your kids are with you, do what you feel is best. My thoughts are: allowing my kids to see me be upset in that moment was true and right. They need to see their mom be upset about being separated from their dad. It helps them learn and understand emotions and that's it's OK to have them, even when you must remain strong. Try to keep it together if you're inside the airport. It makes it harder for them to leave if you're a basket case. Sometimes I sat and watched the plane take off, and other times I left immediately because I was irritated. I associate one song with each deployment, so sometimes I just turned that on, I drove, I sang, and I cried. That day was pity party day. If I had a friend whose husband was on the same team, we'd meet for an early dinner, complain, maybe cry, and drink wine together. I had one deployment where two friends and I had a sleepover with our 8-month-old babies because we didn't feel like going to bed early or being alone. Our husbands left together, and although we all lived on base, we chose not to walk the ONE block back to our own houses and we stayed together for an adult sleepover. Ridiculous you might think, and maybe it was, but I don't care. But don't say ridiculous until you try it. A good sleepover can be a blast.

Once pity party day was over and I woke up the next morning my game face woke up with me. The crying was over; time to grind. There was no time to feel sorry for myself. I had months to get through and I had to fill them with productive things to do. If I didn't, I would sit and think of all the things that could be going wrong where my husband was in the Middle East and that just couldn't be an option.

Some of this list makes you want to cry and the rest make you laugh-cause if you don't. You'll cry. And that's not something we do during deployments and TDYs.

So, without further ado, the three sections of lessons begins.

<u>Preparation for Departure & Things NOT to Do:</u>

- Get Powers of Attorney early, and matter of fact: get them specific (it's literally called a "specific POA" and you'll need several). It's a pain in A to do them once your spouse is gone. A general POA can be almost useless in most situations.

- Make a PCS binder and put EVERYTHING in it. Copies of birth certificates, shot records (people and pets), orders, mail (for proof of address), your resume and references, any moving documents for a moving truck or hired company, receipts, weight tickets, kids' school information, and Powers of Attorney. A binder that can zip shut is great so things don't fall out on accident.

- Carry the binder with you in the vehicle as you travel. Take it to all your appointments once you arrive at the new place and then store it in a safe for the next move.

- Keep it all together, binder or not. It's amazing how you'll randomly need your spouse's social security number, a kid's birth certificate or shot records, and you can't access them.

- Know the passwords to everything; you'll need them.

- Know how to make big purchases; buying or selling cars or houses is difficult if you don't prepare.

- Think months ahead; if tax season is in play, you better gather all that crap before he goes.

- Registering kids for school can be obnoxious when you only have one parent present; get all your documents together.

- If you home-school (we call them the "homies") research your state's laws and requirements for homeschooling. Every state is different, so you need to know what you're getting into.

- If you're SHORT (fun-sized) have your spouse move all the stuff in the top of the cabinets down before they go. You're welcome! Now you don't require a stepladder every time you want a salad bowl!

- Understand that a few weeks prior to their departure they may start to emotionally distance themselves from you. You'll be mad at first until you understand it's the only way they can deal with leaving and not get upset; it's normal.

- Go on dates with your spouse. Dating each other is loving each other. Do this all the time, not just when they're leaving!

- Prepare your kids in an age-appropriate way based on the location their parent will be in.

  - I hung a world map in the hallway by their bedrooms when they were small, and put a pin where dad was. I hung two small clocks next to it to display our time and what time it was where he was, I left a bucket with crayons and paper next to it so they could draw a picture or write a note when they were sad, drop it in the bucket and I would, in turn, either mail those to him or save them for him, I put pictures of them with him on a board next to the map.

  - We had a jar full of chocolate kisses on the table that he had filled in front of them before he left. They each got "a kiss from dad" every night. FOR the LOVE of all creatures if you do this, put more kisses than there are days in the deployment and keep the jar full as you count down. The upside for you here is that when you get to the night before you KNOW he will return you get to eat the remaining chocolate. Again, you're welcome!

- If you have safes of any kind, know the code to them so you aren't locked out.

- Get security cameras up and running around your house.

- Get some home protection equipment like doorstop alarms, self-defense training or devices, window break warnings, and a dog if you see fit (living on base removes some of this).

- Help your spouse pack if it's possible. It is enormously helpful to take the mental load off them, and you will feel more a part of the experience than if you just sit back and watch. The elation you'll feel when they use the stuff you packed that they didn't think about will bring joy to the experience rather than stress and sorrow.

  - I used to pack dryer sheets in his bags so they wouldn't smell bad once he was in his new living situation.

- I got cards and I wrote little notes and had the kids do the same and then I snuck them into his bags, inside his boots, rolled inside clothes, etc. Just little things he could find as he unpacked in the desert.

- Items to pack that he's not thinking about:

  - A collapsible laundry basket

  - Battery-operated string lights or lamp (if they're staying in some sort of tent or box, this makes it a little "homier"

  - A fast-dry towel

  - Two sets of bedsheets

  - Travel chargers

  - A noise-maker for sleep

  - A neck pillow

  - A travel hammock (they can hang it up in the plane).

  - Buy vacuum seal storage bags so you can fit more stuff into the bag. You can buy a memory-foam bed topper and squeeze it into a backpack this way!

  - If he doesn't have any, buy him a pair of noise-canceling headphones; whatever fits your budget. They'll provide privacy in some form or another on the long plane ride to wherever they're going. He'll say he doesn't need them—he does.

  - If you can, buy ALL THE THINGS and return what he doesn't need/want. Load everything into an online shopping cart and just go pick it up, that way you don't even need to load your own car. Just remember to return the unused items ASAP so you don't get stuck with a huge credit card bill!

  - Pack items into packing cubes; one for boxers, one for socks, one for shirts, etc.

- DON'T pack medications into one of those fancy organizers —they'll make him throw them out. If you're packing over-the-counter medications, they have to be in their sealed containers (otherwise, they don't know what's actually in the organizer, thus it's not allowed).

- On that topic, pack Pepto tablets. There's something known as "deployment poops". Maybe from stress, maybe from Middle Eastern food, who knows!?

- Plan a going-away party for your spouse if they're up for it; some hate it, so ask first. Keep it low-key so it's not another stressful thing to accomplish. Plan it a couple of weeks before departure, so they still have the last week with just you, but it gives them a chance to see people they might miss otherwise.

- Have a go bag ready for yourself and your kids in case of an emergency.

- Have an emergency box of supplies ready in case of an emergency or natural disaster in your area while they're away. Trust us here.

- Learn your geographical region and the weather that comes with it. In Alaska, earthquakes may be a thing, but in Florida you need to understand hurricanes and you should have supplies and be ready for all the possibilities.

- Make—with your kids help—a bucket list (ours was called "The Bucket Jar"). Have kids write down things and activities they want to see or do, add your own input and draw one out every weekend while they're gone. It gives the kids input, gives you things to do, and keeps everyone busy.

- Get new windshield wipers; they just might FLY off the car or make it impossible to see mid storm.

- While you're at it get all the vehicles serviced (air in tires, fluids full, etc.) and make sure insurance and registration are good to go, or that you are able to take care of those things.

- When I say take care of the things, don't let the person servicing the car tell you that everything on your car is bad and you need all new filters, brakes, oil, etc. It's probably fine. Just get the oil changed, move on, and ask your husband later.

- If you live in a snowy climate, knowing how to use a snowblower will decrease your chances of extreme arthritis, or make sure you set up help for things like shoveling, snow blowing, battery-jumping, etc.

- Be flexible with holidays and special occasions. Plan celebrations for when he returns or go celebrate it yourself, but don't be mad at your spouse. They're also missing the holiday, anniversary or birthday and NO, it's not their fault. We understand you've spent every Christmas with your family and now they're fourteen hours away and you don't want to travel alone, but you're going to have to get over it. Be flexible, create normalcy for your kids, and try to hide your anger about it all from your kids.

- They miss entire seasons of life. You may spend your first few months as new parents apart, large chunks of your marriage may be spent alone, they may miss your kid's milestone moments, entire sports seasons and chunks of a school year. Do your best to smile and support your kids. Create memories and include your spouse however and whenever possible.

- Unless your home is burning down, somebody died, or you need to pass kid information, DO NOT complain to your spouse while they're gone. A conversation about each other's days is different than constantly complaining about how bad you have it while they're gone, PENDING their location. If they're hanging out in Italy, it's up to you how to vent.

- Stop crying when the actual leaving is taking place. Have some dignity. Cry in the car. You're both sad, give him a pretty face to remember.

- Do NOT ever post dates, times, flight information or locations of your spouse's trips, TDYs and especially deployments. It's a rule, not a suggestion. You can get people killed that way.

## The Situations We Learned From:

- How to give birth without your husband.

- How to help a friend grieve a stillborn child at birth before their spouse could get back.

- How to put a beloved pet down and still maintain your bearings for your kids.

- How to take care of kids that are sick while you're also super sick.

- How to maintain composure when attacks kick off at your husband's location and you don't know if he's alive; you can see the news, but you don't know what's going on.

- How to watch and check the news with caution. Know yourself. (Do you really want to know, or not?)

- How to attend weddings alone, parties alone, dinners alone, and sometimes funerals alone.

- How to buy a house.

- How to buy a car.

- How to sell a car.

- How to sell a camper.

- How to do a claim for a totaled camper that was hit by a tornado while sitting in the RV lot.

- How to potty train. Kids. Dogs. Cats. Just get a fish if you don't have kids. Way easier.

- How to teach kids to walk.

- How to teach kids to talk.

- How to teach kids to read and write.

- How to pick your battles with kids. Your spouse might be deployed, but there's a war raging at home too, and it's your kids testing every boundary you set. Stay strong, friends.

- Don't feel like you have to enforce every single rule and routine that you follow when your family is whole. If you want to let the kids eat in front of the TV sometimes, go for it. It'll help you stay sane and they'll think its fun.

- How to enroll and dis-enroll kids from school in the middle of the school year.

- How to deal with the death of your own friends; suicide is tragic and I wish I had checked on her more.

- How to plan multiple mini vacations for your kids to make the time pass.

- How to plan a massive fourteen day, three state vacation for when it's time for your husband's mid-tour during a remote.

- How to ignore the spouse rumor mill; Get your info directly from him.

- How to drive twelve hours home for Christmas with a dog, two kids and a potty because…potty training.

- How to comfort the youngest kid who is spraying perfume in her eye while you're trying to put lotion on the other kid so your hands are slick and that's not helpful but you still have to calm everyone down.

- How to get the salt out of your kids' eyes because they put chicken nuggets on them and now they're screaming.

- How to deal with your toddler who is obsessed with the coolness of rollie-pollies and earthworms, so she puts them in her pockets cause they're her "friends" and she wants to bring them inside but forgets they're in her pockets and now they're in your washing machine.

- How to live without appliances when they break, so everything comes from a microwave, or you lose everything in your fridge and have to throw it out and buy new. Get renters insurance. Some companies reimburse for food loss in the case of natural disasters where the power is out.

- How to just laugh when you find ammo in your washer and dryer cause your husband was rage packing for his trip and clearly not checking his pockets.

- How to hide in a bathroom as a tornado makes its way past your neighborhood while you're reading books to your kids, so everyone stays calm with a eighty pound dog trying to climb in your lap.

- How to deal with a bomb cyclone once you figure out what it is—and how to get through one—look that up. It was crazy.

- How to live through home repairs like roofing and new drywall, following all the leaks after the bomb cyclone.

- How to climb out a window to shovel because the bomb cyclone created a seven foot tall snow drift against your doors and the garage door is frozen shut.

- How to locate your neighbor's porch furniture from down the street because it's now in your tree in the front yard.

- How to deal with power outages lasting more than a day while you have a toddler and a kid in Pre-K.

- How to have surgery multiple times over the course of several deployments.

- How to treat a dog's skin infection requiring ointment and for the dog to keep a t-shirt on.

- How to adopt a puppy one week before departure, because he's just too cute to pass up and now you're alone with two kids, a dog, and a puppy.

- How to persevere through sickness, all of it, any kind of it, and usually all at once.

- How to help your other friends and co-workers deal with their life stuff while trying to act like you're fine. Dumpster fires are our specialty.

- How to remain durable. You are going to get overwhelmed with the easiest tasks at a moment when you're not prepared. Like, trying to open a bottle of sparkling grape juice on Christmas morning for your kids when he isn't home and you can't get it. Go find a neighbor, they'll do it.

- Weird Fact about me: I hate opening biscuits because I jump when the can explodes. When my husband is gone and I want biscuits….I walk to the neighbor's house and they open it.

- HOW TO ASK FOR HELP! It's really okay! And people want to help you. You have to get over yourself and sometimes kick that pride to the curb.

- How to take care of yourself while they are gone. You cannot pour from an empty cup and trying to muscle through only works for a couple of months. You need consistency in a routine, which helps your sanity.

- How to avoid excitement. (You read that correctly.) Don't tell your kids the date that their parent is coming home, even if you know the date! There are almost always delays and last-minute changes. Just don't tell them. You'll upset them.

- How to manage emotions and help others to. Do NOT put your business on social media. If you and your husband have issues or fight. Go find a therapist in your area. Social media is not your therapist.

- How to use your network. If something breaks in your house, ask another spouse first. They very well may have already learned how to fix it.

- How to wake up at 0500 daily because your animals are used to your spouse feeding them and they're hungry so they won't just go away.

- How to clean it out! THROW AWAY the four boxes sitting in your garage that you've PCS'd with three times and never unpacked. Unpack them and get rid of them!

- And on that note—go through everything when you PCS and if you haven't used it or worn it in more than a year…get rid of it!

- How to decorate your house every time you move and however you want it. Even if you live in base housing or rent. If you like wallpaper, get peel and stick; if you want to paint, do it and just paint it back later. If you wait for your spouse to retire to finally decorate your home the way you love it, you will have wasted twenty years waiting for the perfect house, and by then, your kids will never get to live in a home you made into a home. It's important and it will change how you feel about your space. Don't wait…just decorate!

## "Deployment Certifications"/Resume Additions
## Plus Stuff I Know Only Because I Had To

- Plumbing: faucets and p-traps, toilet bases, shower drains, shower heads, water shut offs.

- HVAC: Change all your air filters in your house regularly, know how to troubleshoot sensors. You'll be happy you learned it the first time a crazy storm or hurricane rolls through and you're A/C won't get your house below eight-five degrees.

- Car mechanic: Yep, I can troubleshoot a 2006 Acura until I learn that the fuse that controls the passenger side window and the fuse that runs the radio will endlessly drain your battery. Took me three new batteries to learn that, but now she cranks every time.

- Drywall installation complete with taping and mudding: cause sometimes folks go through walls.

- Decking: I can build a new deck off the back of the house (with my dad's help).

- Fencing, we can put in new posts and get a new fence up when storms knock them down.

- Painting houses, painting walls, and sometimes just simply painting pictures.

- Postal Service Customs Form Completion Pro: I quite literally taught a class for some spouses early on about how to fill one out and how to mail things overseas.

- Unpacked, moved in, and re-arranged all the furniture in the entire house alone following a PCS because your spouse has to go to work their first weekend you were on station.

- Animal Control: your dogs will always bring you "prizes" cause they're sorry you're lonely, but those prizes are usually dead birds or squirrels and now you have to clean them up.

- Building all the toys and inserting all the batteries on Christmas morning. So long, relaxation!

Again, this list could go on forever. These are just things we personally experienced, some good and some bad. We are stronger for them, and it's made us who we are. You are always more capable than you give yourself credit for.

# 5

## CLUB LANGLEY: ADULT COLLEGE & UNICORN OF THE MILITARY

I arrived in Missouri, unpacked and a month later welcomed my husband home. One of the most surreal homecomings ever. Our kids looked and acted so differently from the last time he'd seen them. He and I had both changed and grown as individuals; he in his prison-like solitude in the Middle East, and I in my circus-like household in Colorado Springs.

Reintegration following deployment is an extremely difficult time. Nobody likes to talk about it—they like to act like it doesn't happen. Just like nowadays when people post all their fantastic news and pictures on social media, but we all know they're falling apart behind the scenes. It's not my style to hide the bad, and I knew reintegration was hard. I mean, this was our fourth and longest separation. We were thick-skinned and battle-tested as a couple at this point. We knew that we'd have about three days of honeymoon phase and then the fighting would begin. It would be like a WWE wrestling match mixed with moments of intense and overwhelming happiness to have each other again. We fought over all kinds of things. You name it! It's up for debate during reintegration. Why do I sleep in the middle of the bed now? Because I could for a year. Why are the kids getting ready for bed so early? Because there has to be an ounce of sanity in the house and that comes when they go to sleep and I'm alone without hearing, "Mama, Mama, Mama." Why in the world are all the dishes, cookware, appliances, etc. on the bottom two shelves of the cabinet? BECAUSE I'm five feet tall and can't reach crap. Literally everything can become an argument. Does it have to? No, but does it? Absolutely. And that's just how reintegration works—it's normal. It's how you come back together as one family living in the same space after months and months apart. Read some of the studies on how families come back together, and kids act out during a parent's imprisonment or release from prison. You'll find some disturbing similarities there.

My husband and I are both heavy on the sarcasm, quick-witted and say-it-like-it-is kind of people. You may have picked up on that by now. It makes for interesting conversation, zingy arguments, and it always makes people wonder if we actually like each other. The thing is, that's how we communicate. He's my God-given soul mate. It's just how we argue. I love a solid quick-witted response during an argument. To the point that mid-debate if a one-liner ran through my head that made me chuckle I was saying it, even if it escalated the debate to an argument. I did it every time. In the middle of an argument once I stopped him and asked, "are you saying stuff to try and hurt my feelings and make me mad?" and he said, "Yep." So, I laughed, and I drew some understanding of him in that moment. It was the moment I realized we were more alike than I originally thought. I admitted how my brain worked in arguments and told him that's why I was throwing out zingers, and we've grown from there. We've even recapped our arguments a few hours later because if you go through them with objective eyes, the point of contention may have been dumb to fight about, but the fight was funny.

It's us. That's how we operate. We don't hate each other. We love each other deeply. We like each other. He's my best friend. We just fight like we're headed into Thunderdome. Go look that up too if you don't know what it is. It'll give you a good mental picture.

We always come back together through reintegration and get ourselves back on track. Reintegration can take a week or it can take a few months. This time it took longer because the separation had been longer, but it's a necessary evil because we're a family.

I started work, he signed into his new squadron and life began in Missouri. Only a few months into that life, things became unhinged as COVID-19 landed stateside and the poop hit the fan. The base had a lot of restrictions as they followed guidelines. COVID meant that for the first time we were living within two and a half hours of family, but we couldn't see them. That lasted for a year, and it sucked. We lived on base, and over the course of the year our neighbors began to PCS and new people began moving in around us. To paint the picture of this neighborhood, you have to understand that we lived at the end of the road with open field behind us in what's referred to as "Senior Non-Commissioned Officer" (SNCO) housing. The only people that lived on our street were people at the enlisted rank of E-7 to E-9, Master Sergeants to Chief Master Sergeants. This group of people, in short, are squadron leaders, charged with managing people, fixing problems and knowing the inner workings of the Air Force. SNCO's a lot of times are workhorses. They're do-ers. They get things done. They like to act on things, not talk about things.

Not all are that way, but the people that moved into the six houses immediately surrounding us were that way and what became of that neighborhood can be described only as: EPIC!

If you have ever attended college or summer camp, you may be able to identify with what I'm about to describe. What took place in that neighborhood isn't unheard of in the military, but it's rare and often only plays out when you're stationed overseas. It doesn't usually encompass such a large group of people, especially one that all live right next door to each other. We couldn't have gotten away from each other if we had tried, so I guess it's good we locked in on one another. Think back to those college or camp days when your friends just barged into one another's rooms at all hours of the day and night and were welcomed, of course, but we implemented a notification system. You walk in and yell "Bing Bong!" and if you got the same in response, you could keep walking. If you heard, "Bong Bing!" you better stop in your tracks and retreat because that meant not everyone was dressed or ready for a visitor.

We all met at a neighborhood BBQ on Memorial Day and the more we talked we realized that we all lived in the six houses that were directly across and beside each other... and even more impressive, we all kind of liked hanging out. That BBQ led to a get-together after the BBQ in one of our front yards, which led to a get-together the next night and from there it took off. That first night we hung out I stood under a streetlight talking with two girls who would become my closest friends (Josey and Pepper, we'll call them) for several hours. We stood under that light swarmed by mosquitoes and just smacking them because we liked each other so much we didn't want to go inside.

Within a week it became almost a daily thing. Friday nights became a standing "date" with the group. If you didn't show, we made sure you knew we weren't impressed with the fact you'd made other plans. We played cornhole—A LOT, but really, we did anything that was competitive. Saturdays were daytime hangouts and sometimes Sunday afternoons. There were 16 of us. This neighborhood became a military family like nothing I had encountered. The most extraordinary part is that all sixteen of us felt that way. This was uncharted territory for everybody, without drama, where we were all comfortable.

I could come home on any given Tuesday after having a crazy, terrible, fantastic, maddening, or sad day at work, and I knew it was going to be OK because a minimum of two of the group would be posted up in lawn chairs in the front yard, usually with a drink in hand ready to welcome me home. It could be any two which is also interesting. We are all married, love our spouses and have solid decade–plus marriages. It could be one of the wives sitting out with another husband that wasn't hers in the front yard just chatting while kids ran around everywhere. Eventually at least six to eight of us would join in, but there wasn't pressure to keep tabs on your spouse because we were all cool and nobody ever tried to make it weird. Everyone was chill, in a great relationship, there to support each other and most of all; NO DRAMA. We rarely took pictures of our activities, we didn't allow videos to be taken, and we were cautious of anyone who joined us for a cornhole tournament or neighborhood hangout that wanted to take photos or videos. We just liked things old school. We lived in the moment. We didn't watch everything that happened through the lens of a phone camera… we were present. We enjoyed our time together so much that we just paid attention to each other. I wish people would return to that because it's an amazing thing… human interaction.

And I'm not trying to be shady, of course we also didn't want pictures and videos cause none of us needed our airmen seeing what we did on our personal time. We did end up being talked about and the airmen said we were famous around base, but the goal was to avoid being infamous.

We designated one of the central houses' front yards and the normal hangout spot. Our street started to look like a campground year-round. There were fire pits out, camping chairs and porch furniture everywhere, speakers and drinks usually out on the porch or in the yard. We became incredibly close in record time. Early on the oldest of the bunch… we'll call him, Pop-Pop decided we needed a group chat so that we could easily say... "I'm going to the yard in ten for whoever's free" and everyone would know. We named that chat Club Langley in honor of the street we lived on. We have (still) team jerseys, our group chat and more stories than I could ever tell. It would be its own book, except—what happened on Club Langley stayed there. Remember, everyone had stressful jobs on a base that had a stressful mission. The ops tempo was insane, and we all needed an outlet.

We found that outlet in each other.

As a group nothing was safe from becoming a competition. One of our most common phrases, which was usually brought up around midnight was.."You wanna race?" That's right. Literally racing… in any form. We raced on scooters and bikes and there were plenty of foot races. Races to see who could run the fastest in sandals or barefoot. Races to see who could get food done first and bring it out and endless physical challenge style competition. Sometimes we raced the kids (I think there were eighteen-ish kids between us all—Jr. Club Langley), sometimes we all decided just the guys needed to race… any race you can think of, we did. We played kickball in the field with the kids and even that became competitive. Cornhole was EXTREMELY competitive. Lots of money changed hands pertaining to cornhole. We competed in board games like sequence, and we even held a tournament once, we had a soup and stew competition, we played the newlywed game for money, (Ahhheem, stands up, clears throat and bows) My husband and I won, of course.

Pop-Pop's house became a designated breakfast destination on Saturday mornings, and the kids loved going to Pop-Pops. We cooked together, ate lots of meals together, spent holiday's together, we went to kids' events together (including one of their weddings), we went through really hard life stuff together, we shared grief when any Airman died together, we celebrated everything possible, and together we lived life in such a way that we were one large family. Dysfunctional, yes, but who doesn't have a weirdo or two in their family anyway?

Did we fight sometimes? Yooooou betcha! But you know what- we still hung out that same day. We excelled at squashing the drama, remembering that we loved each other and just moving on. It was amazing. It's something I pray every military spouse gets to have.

A few things got Club Langley going more than others. I already touched on how we were maniacs when it came to cornhole, but there were so many other things. Fantasy Football put us all in overdrive! We couldn't just have a league and play like normal people.

There had to be stakes and they had to be high.

One Saturday as we sat on the porch squawking about all the random things we sat around and squawked about, Pop-Pop said, "Hey, it's time for football. Who's in and what are we doing?" What he meant was—what's going to happen to the losers and how much money is the winner getting. We talked for a long time about what the stakes would be that year. We came up with the greatest plan. We were going to buy a junk car that was cheap—the goal was $2,000 or less. We were going to make the one guy that wasn't present at the time do the registration for it, because obviously, you snooze you lose! The rules were as follows:

Plan A: The car wouldn't be allowed to be driven off base because, after all, we are civilized and didn't want anyone to get stuck somewhere in it. Each week of football, whoever lost had to drive the car everywhere they went on base: to work, the store, gas station, all of it. The catch was, in addition to the car being a junker, the winner that week got to decorate that car however they wanted as long as it wasn't so crazy we'd get in trouble. It was brilliant! This car would be parked in chief's parking spots, in front of the headquarters building, by the flight line, at the grocery store, and so on. To add to the fun, one of my friends (the very best of friends), Josey from the streetlight, worked from home. She had a fantastic addition to this extravaganza, she'd put an air tag in the car, and then post in our group chat when it was on the move so we could all wave when possible. Some might say this was hazing, but you have to admit that we're creative. We made offers on five cars that night and not a single one came through. It was so upsetting. We were ready for the fun, but the season was starting so we were forced to resort to plan B.

Plan B: The one that worked after the letdown of losing Plan A.

We ordered an adult-size donut costume complete with a headband.

We made a loser sign, complete with lighting that would be placed in the loser's front yard for the week.

The loser each week would get up early on Saturday morning, put on the donut costume, take everyone's coffee order, drive to Starbies, GO INSIDE to pick up the mobile coffee order, take a photo of themselves inside while in the costume.

Next they had to go to the donut shop, GO INSIDE and get donuts for the whole neighborhood, take a picture inside while in the costume, and head back.

All photos had to be posted in the group chat for proof of follow-through. Then they would return to the hood and deliver donuts and coffee to each house in order of who had the most points that week starting with the winner. The pictures are priceless, and of course, we're creative so there was a donut delivery via golf cart, by using a stadium hot dog dealer cart, with and without kids in tow. It got so entertaining that the staff at our local Starbies and local donut dealer started getting in the photos. They waited to see who was coming in each week. Be creative folks! Have a good time with your friends, haze-or don't, but laugh the whole way. And no, I'm not supporting the legit hazing of people. You have one life and if you aren't laughing (in my opinion) you're wrong. You need to find the people that are your people and love them hard with all your might, because you don't know how long you'll have them for.

There are so many stories like fantasy football I could tell, but that's a whole other book. If you've never put a man down a storm drain in the rain to see what's down there at 0100 on a Saturday morning, are you even living?!!! If you haven't set up a canopy in your driveway, put out a rug and outdoor furniture, pillows and blankets and dressed up in costumes to watch Halloween movies with the kids while drinking cider in the fall, have you really watched movies?

OK, since I know you're dying to know. I'll give you one more story. Missouri gets steamy hot in the summers with humidity and heat. It's the humidity that will change your opinion on outdoor shenanigans of ANY kind. So, for the Fourth of July we decided we needed a water slide and a BBQ to make it manageable. Think of scenes from the movie The Sandlot and you'll get what we were going for.

What we landed on was an eighteen-foot-tall water slide that we would set up between my driveway and the neighbor's driveway. We would hook the water hose to my house and the power to theirs. It started out being for the kids and it ended up as a competition for us—are you shocked? We weren't complete savages—the kids got it all morning, took a break for lunch so we could slide and then got it again on day one, but day two that slide became the adults slide after lunch. As we all sat in the driveway we came up with an obstacle course involving the slide. We would do it in bracket style and we were in teams of two. We drew names from a cup for teams, and you were not allowed to be a team with your spouse. I drew my partner and low and behold... I drew the guy that was the genesis of all the street races and the instigator of the group! But he didn't always win, bless his heart. We'll call him Obie. Now, I love Obie and his family as much as everyone else, but sometimes his drive to compete overshadowed the fact that maybe he wasn't as good as he thought at the task that was at hand. And now, he had me as a teammate. I'm extremely competitive, but I'm broken. I'd had nine total orthopedic surgeries at this point in my life including a total knee replacement. I'm determined and I don't give up, but I'm not fast by any means. He and I decided that we were going to own the dumpster fire we were in and go for the gold, baby!

GAME ON.

As a group we went through lots of ideas the day prior about what should be a part of this relay. We even considered folding a fitted sheet as part of the course. I would have lost it for us right there. We landed on starting by taking a shot. We followed the shot by flipping a cup to land it right side up. Once you landed the cup you had to run across the street where there was a basketball goal and a designated line drawn from which you had to shoot, and you couldn't leave that station until you made a basket. If you made the basket, you would run back across the street, climb the inflatable ladder to the water slide, go down, get off the slide, and head to the sidewalk. On the sidewalk, you placed a potato (that's right...a russet) between your knees and walked down the sidewalk where you had to drop the potato into a five gallon bucket, then tag your partner who would complete the same entire process.

WHEEEW!

Remember what I said about it being a bracket? Well, if you won, you got a five minute break before the next round. You had to win five rounds to be the champ. Once Obie and I made it through the first couple rounds that was it. We HAD to be the champions. We were pep talking each other, telling the other teams they were going to lose—lots of smack talk with Club Langley all the time. There we stood at the end, drenched, out of breath after five rounds, and just proud as punch cause WE WON BABY!!!!

Maybe you're wondering what the winner got? Trophies of course!

That's enough of the stories but just know that we had so much fun and were so close that airmen started asking me at work if Club Langley was real because they'd heard of us or driven by to see if we were doing anything crazy.

We all worked so hard in a stressful environment and were all in different squadrons, but we took care of airmen and their families like nobody else did. We came together and let the situations and environment forge a family of sixteen. We worked out the problems of our piece of the Air Force on our base in the front yard on Friday nights sometimes because it was the right thing to do. The level to which these friends would show up is unmatched. It's once in a lifetime and I'm forever thankful that God chose to send us to Missouri instead of Alaska. There's nothing that could replace the people and the memories I have of Club Langley.

# 6

## THE PCS THAT SAVED MY LIFE

*This chapter is dedicated to my case manager, Sharon, for her tireless dedication to sticking with patients all the way, for never giving up on us, for being our cheerleader & advocate, and for getting us through the stress and difficulties associated with establishing care.*

Seasons come and go. We knew PCS season was coming. We knew we would all receive orders for various reasons, and knowing that it was coming to an end was painful. In the military, the bittersweet emotions that come with a piece of paper are hard to describe. Excitement is in the air, and the next chapter in a new place is approaching, but confronting your own thoughts and feelings about starting over may be awful. As a spouse, the process can consume you. You may become unemployed, you don't have friends, and you won't report to work right away. By the end of the first week, your active duty spouse will know people, be employed, and may even make plans for you with new people from work. Your entire life picks up, and you begin again. The older you get, the harder that gets. You don't want new friends—you want your friends. Everyone you meet has a different background and experience, and you're searching to find the same connections that you had before. Recreating what you loved at the previous base is almost impossible. But you need to keep going—make forward progress, so you hold your head high and make the best of the place you're in.

Orders started rolling in. The only comfort we found in that process was that all six houses would be PCSing within one hundred days of each other. Nobody was going to be left behind in the neighborhood to try to rebuild what once was—we would all move on together. It's EXTREMELY hard to be the last one on the block when the block was so memorable. You sit and watch people move in, hoping they'll want to hang out and that they have kids, and it can be disappointing. So, at least no one would be left behind. It's kind of a fairytale ending to that kind of unicorn experience.

Our final event with everyone, we decided, would be a house crawl. It was dual-purpose. Hang out together and have fun, of course. But it also allowed us all to clean out the fridge and pantry so we could start packing. Each house had to have a snack and a drink, and maybe a quick game, then we'd go to the next house. We even had a house where we played a table ping pong game, but we filled the cups with water and electrolyte packs. I told you we were responsible! Such a fantastic final event to close out our time and stand down the physical Club Langley.

Our orders dropped, and we were moving to Georgia. The funny thing about Georgia is that my husband, throughout the years, had clicked the volunteer button for a specific unit in Georgia. He'd clicked it twenty-plus times, but we'd never gotten it... odd. That unit always needed people—deployable people, which was his wheelhouse. He had five deployments under his belt, and yet, nothing until now, late in his career. At this point, he was getting older, and his body wasn't held together with the same young guy glue it used to be. He has that unresearched dad strength; he's in good shape, but the thought of potentially jumping out of planes and doing the deployment training for this particular unit sounded like it could be difficult for a "well-used" guy.

Time for big girl undies again.

We prepared to move in the thousand ways you have to prepare. The time to depart was near, and we began loading our moving truck. On day two of loading, as we went up the loading ramp with a workbench, it shifted and hit me in the chest. WOW, I thought. That hurt more than expected. Like, sheeeeesh. It took my breath away.

See, a few months prior, I noticed a little marble-sized knot on the left side of my chest. It was almost touching my sternum. I told Josey about it, and she was, and is still, my voice of reason. She told me I needed to go get it checked. It was, after all, in my left breast. I was great at taking care of others' medical needs as part of my job, but not great at addressing my own. She stopped me in the middle of my list of excuses on why I didn't need to go to the doctor and said, "If one of your patients came to you with this, what would you do?" She was right. I would make them see someone. I had recently seen a doctor and had a partial hysterectomy scheduled for the week following this conversation, so I told her I would draw a line around it and bring it up. I followed through with drawing the line, but when I got to the pre-op appointment, the knot had gone down, and I was struggling to feel it. The doctor felt around it and said if it returned, let her know or tell someone at our new base. She knew I was PCSing, so I would have to get new doctors at the next location. I didn't think about it again after that. It basically went away for the next five months, bringing me up to loading the truck.

On the moving truck, I began to feel around, and it was painful. There it was. The knot had returned. Again, the size of a marble, but now it was sore and hurt to touch. I told my husband, who immediately said, "Do you want to call the doctor and get that checked?" I thought about it and decided I would wait until we arrived in Georgia. We were only two weeks away from our arrival, and if this knot turned out to be something, they could cancel our PCS. I remained quiet.

The evening of September 10th arrived, and we pulled into our new neighborhood in Georgia. Off base this time, and we bought a house. It's late afternoon, and we were arriving within a week of a hurricane blasting through our new town. We didn't know if our house had damage, power, or even water—we were just praying it was livable. It was in good condition with very minor damage. We had power! We couldn't get our A/C to cool below eighty-five degrees in the house, but we had a house, and the A/C was fixable in a few days' time!

Unloading our vehicles and the small trailer we brought with us began. I noticed my heart rate was fluctuating fairly dramatically for no reason identifiable to me. I was having heart palpitations, and when standing still, my heart rate would go from 70 to 120, then drop again. I was tracking it on my watch, trying to manage it and calm myself down.

Could I be stressed more than normal and just not noticed?

Our moving truck would be dropped off in a couple of days, and I was concerned that I wouldn't be able to help unload for fear of passing out. The next afternoon, my mom arrived, and since she would be with our kids, I decided to go to the Emergency Room. Things weren't improving; Josey's words were in the back of my head telling me to get checked, and my husband was echoing Josey's comments. I thought I potentially had an infection. I assumed I'd go in, they would check my heart, and I'd leave with antibiotics or be told I was stressed. I was not prepared for what was to follow.

We sat in the ER, waiting to be called back. My first round of basic heart tests was complete. I mentioned that I had a lump near my sternum that I thought could be the cause of an infection or something. It was the first time I had used the word lump. It felt scary to say. I really didn't think it was anything, but still, deep down, I didn't have the warm fuzzies about it. They called me back to a room after more tests, and the doctor came in. She was awesome. Immediately, she had a calming presence, which was nice in an ER in a brand-new state. She said, "Do you like straightforward kind of information?"

"Yeeees?" I replied, cautiously.

"OK", she said. "There's no good way to say this, so here we go. Your CT shows a mass in your left breast that the radiologist and I are confident is breast cancer. Now I can't tell you that with 100% certainty, but you need a mammogram, an MRI, and to see a surgeon and oncologist very soon. You're young, I don't want you to panic. I'm going to do everything I can to get you referrals and get things started for you. What you cannot do is wait."

There are no words to describe the gut-punch feeling that comes when you hear the word cancer. The air leaves the room, and it takes all joy with it. It feels like you're sitting in a vacuum and there's no way out. In a single moment, your life becomes different, forever. We didn't even speak. We just stared at the floor and periodically looked at each other before staring at the floor again.

What was there to say?

How would we say it?

What about my kids?

How bad is this?

What from hell is happening?!

I did not cry. I did not have the emotions to even panic; I just sat there hearing her tell me what the first steps in the process would be, but I wasn't listening. My brain felt like one hemisphere turned itself completely off, and the other hemisphere was out picking daisies. Nothing made sense. Why was this happening? Where was God when I needed him the most?

I'll tell you where God was. He was right in the middle of it, ready and waiting to hold my hand and guide me. Sitting in that ER at 0200, I texted the only person aside from my husband I could think of who would lift my spirits, even though I knew she was sleeping. I texted Josey and told her what I'd just heard. I wanted her to wake up to the sound of her phone, but it was the middle of the night so I tried not to get my hopes up. In the early morning hours, she texted me back knowing that I probably couldn't handle a phone call. I was admitted into the hospital by the time I heard from her, and I was relieved when I saw it was her. She knows me so well. It was as if we had been friends our whole lives, and she had become more like blood than friend. My husband and I couldn't comprehend what was coming, and he was processing just like I was. We both needed the calming words of an objective party.

The next day, I was released from the hospital. I had a lot to do. Our insurance hadn't even moved us over from one state to another yet. I didn't have a doctor in Georgia, and yet I needed so many referrals. I spent hours on the phone with insurance, trying to send things through and get assigned a provider. This was where I saw God's hand at work first. I got the kindest man on the phone with insurance, and while it took a few hours, he made it all happen.

There was NO WAY I was telling my kids until I knew for sure what I was dealing with. School had already started in Georgia. They had kid stress to contend with. Starting a new school, making new friends, and beginning their lives again in a new place. We talked with my mom while they were at school to try to digest what the plan was and what we would do. I went to a few appointments locally and met with some great doctors. During that first week, so much happened that it felt like I lived in a snow globe that a toddler had just stolen from their sibling and was running rampant with. I met with the local general surgeon, whom I really liked, and he confirmed that it was, in fact, breast cancer. He didn't know the type or stage yet, but I needed surgery. I left the first appointment with him and had another appointment in a few days for clarity on my biopsy, which would give us a treatment path to start with. In those few days, God really began to work. He had his hands in things I can only see looking back, right down to the timing of our PCS. It had been moved up, and it turned out to be perfect.

My mom had returned home with the intent to come to Georgia once we had a strategy. After my first round of appointments was complete, my mom called me and said, "There's an MD Anderson Facility in Florida, and it's only two hours from you. Please consider going there."

Don't forget—I'm a Texan, and what we know as the gold standard for cancer treatment and research is MD Anderson. There are many great cancer facilities, but this was the one I had always known best. This was a facility in another hospital system, but was part of the MD network. I was slightly irritated because I wanted this to end already, and calling them for an appointment might take forever. Within an hour, my step-mom texts me and it says, "Hey, I have a cousin who did residency at the MD Anderson facility in Florida, and it's close to you. Would you consider going there?"

Okay, God. Now I'm fully irritated because, again. I'm trying to do this quickly here at home so that I don't put extra strain on my husband and kids, and maybe I can just be done with it.

Thirty more minutes go by. Ping! My dad texts me. It says, "There's an MD close to you. You need to go there."

I became so frustrated that I stood up and said out loud, in my living room by myself, "God, why? What do you want me to do?! Everyone wants me to go somewhere else, and I just want it to end. What do I do?"

I meant every one of those questions in a challenging way. I'm pretty sure my hands were swinging and, if you're familiar with the knife hand, just know that was going strong too.

As I lowered myself back down on the couch, it was as if the trip from standing to sitting was a thousand-year journey. By the time my butt hit the cushion, my whole heart flipped. I became overwhelmed by peace and calm. Instantly, I knew that I had to go to MD. I couldn't even figure out why I'd questioned my thoughts about it or why I'd challenged God with questions he already had the answers to. There wasn't anything wrong with the facilities here in our new city, but I didn't know them the way I knew MD. Again, I could hear Josey saying, "What would you tell your patient to do?"

Now I had the daunting task of looking a doctor in the face whom I liked and asking him to send me somewhere else. I went to my appointment with him the next week, and I sat feeling so guilty and ashamed as I prepared to ask him for a referral. I respected and had faith in him; he had great bedside manner, he delivered life-altering news to me in a sensitive, caring way, and I am forever grateful to him. He began to talk to me about surgery options, and I finally just spit it out, "I really appreciate you, and I don't want you to take this the wrong way, but I'm a Texan, and MD Anderson is what I know. I've only lived here for thirty-six hours and just want to be somewhere I'm comfortable. Would you be willing to give me a referral there?" He calmly and in a comforting way said, "Yeah, I can do that for you. It's not a problem. I'll go do your referral now, and you let me know if you need me." Classy, professional, and caring is what that man was and is. He's the true definition of what doctors should strive to be. In that moment, he heard me. He saw me. He put my care and treatment plan in the hands of others because he knew it comforted me. He's clearly someone born to be a doctor who found his calling, even though he wasn't going to be my doctor for the whole treatment.

I'd followed my gut to this point, and now I had to play the waiting game for an appointment. MD Anderson called me the following morning and said they had a slew of appointments for me in three weeks' time. All the appointments would be on the same day, and they had squeezed me into the schedule because I was thirty-eight years old and they needed to get treatment going quickly.

Three weeks? Threeeee WEEKS?!

That seemed SOOOO long to wait, but in the grand scheme, and looking back, I could see that I'd probably had cancer for six to eight months and hadn't known that's where my issues were coming from. I had been fatigued beyond explanation for no reason and had found the lump six months prior. So, I just had to tell myself that it was only three more weeks. My new goals were to get up every day, smile, and not let the enemy steal my joy. I had kids to take care of and love, and a husband who was quickly trying to sign into his new squadron so he could fill his commander in and get his head in the caregiver game.

The wait felt like an eternity. MD had me complete my biopsy that the local doctor had already ordered, so that broke up the waiting a bit, and it felt productive to at least get the biopsy done. I knew it would be ready by the time I got to my appointment, and then MAAAAYBE the oncologist would have everything she needed to tell me everything I wanted to hear. I was ready to hear that this was stage zero or one, an easy fix—we do surgery, and I move on with life.

That's what everyone wants to hear.

All cancer patients are forced into a lifetime membership of a club we never asked to join. Cancer is a marathon, an ultra-marathon. It never ends. Just because your initial, acute treatment ends doesn't mean it's over. It's NEVER over. It's a lifetime of worry about recurrence, medicine to take, appointments to have, and so many other things. Yet, we must be active members if we want to live, have longevity, and rebuild our quality of life.

*The Talk*

During the wait, we decided it was time to tell my kids. They were going to have to know, and I don't like hiding things from them. Everyone has their own style of parenting, so hear me when I say—these were our choices, and I respect a parent's right to choose. Military kids are exposed to things in life that make them cultured, mature, and, in my opinion, most times more well-rounded. Sometimes the things they're exposed to aren't all rainbows, cupcakes, and fairy tales. They're exposed to death and sometimes, unfortunately, that means death of their friends, parents, or their own parents, deployments, long stretches of time where they have to act more grown than they are; even if you try to shelter them from it. They experience lots of moving, starting over, learning to adapt, and make new friends everywhere they go, and the list goes on. The way we parent is open and honest. We don't hide things from our kids, and we don't shelter them from what the world holds. Don't get me wrong here—we filter it down to an age-appropriate level, but I'm not trying to put a cherry on top of everything I say to them. They must learn to deal with hard things in life, so we knew—

It was time that they knew.

It was the first time I teared up, and it was the hardest talk I've ever been a part of. It wasn't really much of a conversation. We sat them down on the couch and told them we had something very serious to tell them. I started by telling them that I was sorry, that I wished I wasn't having to add one more thing to their plates since we just moved, but that I would always keep them informed. I told them that I had gone to the doctor because I was worried about a little knot in my chest, and that the doctor told me that it was cancer. Before I could continue, my youngest daughter burst into tears and came to lie on and hug me. It overwhelmed me with sadness. I couldn't fight back tears, and truth be told, I'm crying as I write this. As I hugged her, I looked at my older daughter. She was sitting quietly, staring at the floor with a look of shock and anger on her face. She wasn't crying or talking. I asked her if she understood and if she was OK. She just said yes and asked if she could go to her room. While it hurt a little bit that she wanted to go to her room and appeared as if she was fine, I knew that she wasn't, and I told her she could go. My husband told her that everything was going to be OK and that we would come check on her in a few minutes. She said OK and off she went. She's a lot like me. She has my traits when it comes to dealing with emotions, which is usually not dealing with them. I'm the queen of lack of emotion... or at least display of emotion. I'm great at just locking it up, putting my brave face on, and pressing. I knew she got that from me, so I tried to think of how I would react in this situation when I was eleven years old. Exactly the same way.

While the oldest processed things in her room on her own, the little one struggled. We got her calm enough to talk, and I asked her, "Do you know what cancer is, hun?" She said through her tears in her little shaky voice, "No, I just know it's scary. Are you going to die?"

Ugggghhh, this kid was making me feel feelings, and I didn't like that!

The poor baby was just terrified, and it broke my heart. I told her that it makes me sick and there's something wrong with the cells in my body, but that I had very good doctors and would be seeing them soon, so I could get all the answers for her. I told her I wasn't going to die anytime soon and that I would update her all the time so she would know what was going on. That seemed to comfort her. She got down and went and crawled into her dad's lap. My husband is her safe zone. Heck, he's my safe zone. While the older kid is just like me, the younger one is a daddy's girl. She just sat with him for a long time while he hugged her.

Eventually, I asked her if she wanted to go play or color, and she said yes and went to her room to color. We checked on the older kid, and she was OK. I gave her the same speech I'd given the younger one and told her it was going to be OK. I left them both to process in their own ways while we retreated back to the living room. That conversation lives in my head. I can recall it like it was yesterday, and it'll never leave me. My kids were forced to grow up that day in a way I didn't want them to.

We finally arrived at what I call "MD Day". In my head, it was go time. I was ready for a fight. I can be scrappy, spicy, feisty—whatever you want to call me, but you won't ever get the opportunity to call me a quitter. It's not who I am.

To this point, the only time my eyes had gotten wet was when we talked to my kids. This wasn't the time to cry; I didn't have time to be upset or feel sorry for myself. It was time to SEND IT! All of it. Time to get after this bodily invasion with everything I had.

My husband and I checked in at MD and were immediately taken back behind the check-in desk to a private room. Every person working in this hospital is the nicest human you've ever met. The sweetest lady talked to us, told us she was going to pass us off to my nurse navigator, and she handed me "The Binder." I thought, Wow. This is very organized. This binder had everything in it, down to what hotels and restaurants were closest if I needed to stay during treatment. There were several dividers with sections for appointment notes, a calendar to write appointments, a sheet to place business cards, a section for survivorship information, and resources. I remember thinking—

Am I seriously going to need all this? Seems like it might be overkill.

FAMOUS. LAST. WORDS.

My face talks a lot, even when my mouth doesn't move. You may be familiar with that lack of stoicism in people you know. My husband questioned me as we walked to the elevator about my face when I looked at the binder. I told him my thoughts, and he took the binder from me. "I'll take notes for you so you can just listen," he said. Good plan, I thought. I figured we wouldn't have much use for it.

Gaawwhhhleee, was I wrong!

The appointments came at me like the whack-a-mole game. Just one after the next, enormous amounts of information, decisions to make, and testing to do. On that first day, I attended three appointments: breast oncology, breast oncology surgery, and plastic surgery. The oncologist had scheduled me for five more tests and blood draws to complete that day, and all the while, my husband was taking notes fast and furious.

They laid out all my options based on my biopsy. I learned that I was Stage Two (tentatively). I would only know for sure after surgery. I learned I had the most common type of breast cancer (IDC or Invasive Ductal Carcinoma) and that I was ER/PR+, HER2-, but that I had the most aggressive form of it, known as grade 3. Grade 3 moves quickly, meaning the most urgent test I would complete that day was my PET scan to see if it had spread. The ER/PR+, HER2—speaks to hormone receptors. In simple terms: estrogen was not my friend and in fact was feeding my enemy...

Rude, but OK, time to deal with it.

I was more overwhelmed than I had ever been, and trust me, I'd been in some situations. I was trying to remember everything they told me, gather all the information, run up and down between floors of the hospital to accomplish tests. It was whipping my butt.

I mean. Thank the Lord for THE BINDER, right?!

My husband had that thing on point. He put everyone's business card in there, wrote down all my appointments in the calendar, gathered all the paperwork, and took notes. My oncologist, bless her heart for real, wrote everything down for me because I told her I was a visual learner (amazing that she even asked!), and then she gave me the paper so I would have it for reference.

The PET scan that afternoon covered my whole body. We could see it on the screen as it scanned. The anxiety was high, watching to see if I lit up anywhere else. I was lying still on the table and praying that the Lord wouldn't have me looking like a fully lit Christmas tree on the screen. The scan took about forty-five minutes, and thirty minutes in, the lady doing the scan asked me if I'd ever had jaw surgery. Weird, I thought, and no. I hadn't ever had anything done to my jaw. She asked me again, "Have you ever had a jaw injury, or broken that bone? Maybe you had some dental work done?" I panicked inside. She was asking because my lower jaw was completely lit up on the screen. She told me sometimes it lights up old injuries, so if I couldn't think of anything happening to it and it wasn't painful, I shouldn't worry too much. She said the oncologist would review it, but that when cancer is in a bone, it usually becomes painful. This was the first big secondary scare of my process.

My next appointment to review all the tests was the following week. The oncologist started me on a chemo pill that I would start taking immediately. It was to hopefully reduce the tumor size before surgery and start turning off the estrogen that was driving this crazy train.

We started the two-hour drive home, going over everything we'd learned, trying to make sense of it, discussing all the options for surgery and planning how we would make it all work. We literally didn't know a SOUL in our new city. But as military families do, we settled on: we'll figure it out. Over the course of that week, I began to have lots of lower back pain, not in my bones, but my kidneys were killing me! So much that it kept me awake. I went to urgent care—finally—and naturally, when it rains, it pours, doesn't it?! I had a kidney infection from all the nasty barium I drank to complete the tests at the hospital. They had warned me that it was possible, and I had done the tests anyway. Now, here I was, one week into my initial treatment phase and on antibiotics.

Truly winning.

Through the weekend, we continued discussing options, doing our research, consulting people who had more knowledge than we did, and formulating a plan. The oncologist had already told me that she wasn't sure if Chemotherapy would be part of the plan yet. She wouldn't know that until she had the DNA from the tumor and looked at all the tests and scans. I just kept thinking maybe I could get out of this without dreaded chemo, and it wouldn't be so bad, but we had to plan for all the what-ifs. It's a weird time to live in when you're between those types of appointments. We, as a society, are always trying to teach people not to harp on the "what-if" situations—to live in the moment here and now that you have control of, and yet, there we were. Forced to consider the "what -if" because we had no plan for the care of our kids!

My husband went to his new squadron and signed in, immediately meeting with the commander. For context, it's important to know that the squadron he was originally assigned to at this new duty station changed when we were one week away from departing Missouri. It's not terribly uncommon at this duty station, but my husband was high-ranking enough that they didn't swap as much, so it was a small surprise. That turned out to be a blessing because the commander he got when we arrived was who we needed for the life we were currently living. My husband came home from that meeting and said, "Okay. I talked to my leadership. They said they'd see me next month and once I had more information about your treatment, they said they'd adjust my schedule as needed, but for now I have the month off to get through this initial phase."

I MEAN...

SHOCK and AWE. It absolutely blew my mind.

The military can be a rough place. The mission is first, always. And honestly, I get it. It's the nation's business of war and protection for the homeland. I'm for it. That mission is important, and I understand it. It must be done. In past years, we had a commander who always said, "Mission First, People Always." While I understood what he meant, I guess I just never fully grasped what that looked like in real time. I loved that commander dearly. He was one of the best human beings I've ever known. I think because I was doing okay at the time we were under his command, it wasn't being applied directly into my life, and now it was. We were living in the moment where the "People Always" half of that motto was being executed by a completely different guy, and I have deep appreciation for him. My husband was going to have a whole month with me to develop our plan, unpack our house, cause that was still a thing, help get our kids settled, give them some stability, and be there with me while the unknown ate me alive. It's the fastest and most efficient we've ever unpacked and set up a house. I guess I knew the clock was ticking.

Within two weeks, the whole thing was done. The stuff hung on the walls, boxes broken down and given away to other military spouses, the yard set up, kids' rooms decorated, all of it. I was irritated with myself that it had taken cancer to get me to move with urgency and get this house made into a home. Like, come on, girl, get it together. Could have been doing it this way the whole time!

I got into Club Langley chat, and I broke the news to everyone since Josey had been the only one to really know the details of what was happening. Josey was my best friend. I kept her in the loop every day, and she always responded with support and words of encouragement, but not cheesy quotes and phrases that would have irritated me. She encouraged me in the way I needed it. I needed jokes, laughter, and random memories of Club Langley. I wanted life updates on her family, too—normal stuff. I craved normalcy, and she knew that without me having to tell her. We discussed hard stuff too, but only when I wanted to, and she didn't push me. There weren't a bajillion questions because she knew I didn't have answers. The Club Langley ladies all got into our separate ladies chat and daily sent me positive thoughts, checked on me, and asked how they could help. It kept me going. They're true friends, and I knew they weren't going to leave me hanging or cancer ghost me.

The diagnosis phase before treatment kicks off is purgatory. There's some information, but not enough to know what will happen. There's tentative planning that must take place, but the dates?—We'll get back to you with the dates. There are people you want and need to tell, but you don't feel like you're ready because you can't answer questions, and there will be

So. Many. Questions.

Six months prior, a close friend of mine, a colleague and teammate at work, was diagnosed with stage 4 lung cancer. He was healthy, he is young, didn't smoke, worked out regularly, and he was on active duty for crying out loud. He had joined the cancer club that nobody wants to join. He PCS'd before finding out and texted me to break his news. I went out to my truck one day, checked my phone, and had a very long text from him. He said he didn't want me to find out on social media, but he didn't think he could call me and get the words out, so he'd settled on texting. I ugly cried in my truck for a long time. Shock and anger filled the cab of the truck. I was now facing the same news, but at the time, I had no idea what was coming. His text read like and felt like a goodbye text. Like he needed to get it all out in case things went bad, fast. I physically felt sick; my chest was so heavy with anxiousness. I don't recall my exact words in response. It was a blur, but I know I started with not liking the tone he took when writing like it was a goodbye. I told him that it was time to fight and that I didn't want to have to go all the way to Colorado just to smack him so he'd remember who he was, and that he cannot just give up. Our relationship was somewhat like siblings, and he's one of the biggest pranksters I've ever had the pleasure of knowing, so that's the tone I took. I went at him like he was my brother who needed a talking to.

Now here I was, six months later, and in the same club. I let him know what was happening, but I intentionally made sure it didn't read like a goodbye text. I couldn't allow him to tell me I was doing the same thing I'd told him to stop. If I'm being honest, though, I'd already considered my own death multiple times at this point. Stage 2 may not sound bad to the common person who knows nothing about cancer and how staging works, but grade 3 and the word aggressive weren't giving me good juju vibes. He, of course, was supportive, told me how his treatment was going, we exchanged questions and answers, and promised to keep each other up to date.

This phase remained weird. It had to. What else was it going to be until I had more to go on? Thankfully, the next appointment came, and we moved from a crawling to walking. MD Day #2 was upon us. The drive to MD was tense, but quiet. My husband and I talked on and off, but we both sat in our thoughts most of the ride. We knew it was decision and information time, and it could be good or bad, but no matter what, it was time for action.

# 7

# STRENGTH, GRIT, AND MASTECTOMY PJS

My oncologist walked in with her calming presence, warming smile, and soft approach. She sat down and dove right in. The nurse navigator is in the room, taking notes and helping plot the attack plan. She starts with, "Your PET scan looks pretty good."

Whew! One hurdle to be cleared.

"There is a spot on your chin that is lit up that I'm not sure what that is, but it doesn't look like cancer to me from the scan." She questions me about prior injuries and dental work.

Uh oh. I couldn't recall anything. I'd been an athlete my whole life, I'd played softball for many years, and I had, in fact, been hit in the face by a ball before. I caught and had the mask rubbing on my chin, I ran cross country and had fallen fairly hard in races a couple of times, and I'd lifted weights for many years. I'm not so proud that I can't admit that I had absolutely hit myself in the face with the bar doing Olympic lifts before. Embarrassing, but truthful. I told her everything, and she felt that it had probably caused the mark on the scan. She just asked that I see a dentist at some point and have them double-check.\

One more appointment to add to the endless list of appointments.

While she didn't see any cancer in my lymph nodes on the scan, that doesn't always remain true once surgery is complete. Sometimes it's just too small for the scan to pick up. For now, she felt good about it and didn't see any noticeable metastasis.

Wheeeew! Huge win!

There was no spread thus far, but now things felt urgent. She began to lay out the plan. She asked if I had decided on surgery and if I was seeing both surgeons that day. "Yes to both. I was to stay on the chemo pill until surgery, and once she had the tumor removed, DNA and lymph nodes removed and checked, we would have the answer on chemo. In order to keep the cancer from metastasizing, the process needed to begin quickly. She said, "You are young, we must move quickly. Before this cancer gains the ability to spread. I will do everything I can do, and I will use the most up-to-date research for your treatment, but I need you to take care of yourself, mind, body, and spirit. This fight is a marathon, not a sprint. I believe at this point, I can use the word curable, but that only comes with a long-term plan. I will see you after surgery to go over it. Good luck with surgery."

I remember that appointment well. There was no time for sugar coating; there was only time for transparency and treatment progression. She delivered scary information as if she were telling me I had a cold, and she was going to send over a script for cough medicine. Calm, cool as the backside of the pillow, and with an authority of certainty that created a sense of peace in me.

Next up: Breast Oncology Surgeon.

Here we go. It's game time. Let's do this. In the first appointment, she presented my surgery options. I could do a lumpectomy, but it would certainly require radiation if I chose lumpectomy. I could do a single mastectomy and only remove the left breast, or I could do a double mastectomy. She covered all the research and what the studies showed. Lumpectomy, to me, was out of the question.

Before you go any further, I must remind you that these choices are deeply personal and every cancer patient makes a different choice based on their beliefs, their own mental health, and what they think is right for them. These are MY choices and the reasons behind them.

I knew that plenty of people had lumpectomies with radiation and came out fine, but it felt wrong. I'm relying on my gut (aka Holy Spirit-led guidance), and my gut reminded me that the most recent four women I knew of who had lumpectomies had all passed away. It felt wrong, it would leave me with breast tissue—left and right side—that I had before, and I didn't trust it. Matter of fact, I didn't trust 'em at all! These things had betrayed me and allowed cancer in.

They had to go.

Single mastectomy seemed somewhat logical, except cosmetically, it appeared that surgery could be a difficult road ahead. The surgeon told me that in the 90s, a law was passed that provided "the right to be symmetrical," and with that, I could also opt for a double mastectomy. I had no faith in the right side at this point anyway. I knew the double mastectomy was a big surgery, but for my own mental health, it was the way I could have some peace knowing I'd removed all the tissue.

During that initial waiting period, I did bloodwork and met with a genetics counselor to review it. I had the option to have them only check the genes that led to breast cancer and a couple of other women's cancers, an option for them to check forty-seven genes and all forty-seven of those have treatment that exists, or I could have them check all ninety-six cancer genes. The problem with the ninety-six is that there isn't treatment for all of those types of cancer, so did I really want to know if I had the gene, also knowing there wouldn't be treatment?

I didn't; I went with forty-seven. Check all my genes that you can check for cancer, where there could be treatment provided. And guess what! All forty-seven are in perfect working order. All of them. Even the ones that cause breast cancer. It seemed my cancer was deemed sporadic or environmental.

With that knowledge, I had lost faith in keeping any breast tissue cause who knew what it would do if I left it there! In addition, I knew my tumor was almost touching my sternum. It was extremely close to the bone and my heart and lungs. I needed to know it couldn't get to those.

It's easy to judge a person's choice in surgery when you aren't the person. I'm sure surgeons even think to themselves: the research says it's the same outcome if you just do the lumpectomy. But it's NOT THE SAME IN YOUR MIND. What brought me comfort was that I didn't feel pressured at all to choose one over the other. She just provided me with the options and said, "You have a week to think about it, but you have to tell me what you want to do when I see you next week." So, with that, I had researched for hours and hours and ultimately knew I was doing a double mastectomy.

I gave her my choice, and she launched right into how surgery would go. She would have a surgical partner with her; she would remove the cancer side plus three sentinel lymph nodes to be tested for cancer. Her partner would remove the non-cancer side, and then the plastics team would put me back together. Well, that was easy. I expected much more of a back and forth. She knew I was going to see the plastic surgeon next and said she would link up with him after to get the date confirmed.

I met with the plastic surgeon, who created even more decisions to make. I didn't know this was such an involved process. He presented multiple options for surgery to include: expanders, implants, a procedure known as a DIEP flap that used your own tissue for reconstruction, and he gave all the details for each.

Ladies, it's an interesting appointment with your husband sitting in the corner while you stand with your arms outstretched, no clothes on your top half, a surgeon taking measurements and feeling around while he talks through the plan. Don't get me wrong, it was professional and he's a phenomenal surgeon, but it's still awkward to say the least. Just picture it, and if you giggle, you understand. This guy does this all day, every day, but here I was laughing and being a weirdo while I'm sure he was thinking, "gawwwlee, lady, I'm just trying to make you look normal after they do the life-saving stuff." Either way, I laughed uncomfortably the whole time.

I have to leave a little of the unknown, so I'm keeping the type of surgery I chose to myself. Sorry, but not sorry.

He said they would call me with a surgery date because it required coordinating an operating room, and he would also be bringing in partners to assist him with the surgery. That call came a week later, and I was going to have to wait five more weeks for surgery. They had booked an O.R. for me, and it would be mine for 10 hours. There would be between four and six surgeons and Physician Assistants working on me throughout the day, and it just took five weeks to align all the schedules.

Frustration was mounting, but it also gave me time to prepare. I scheduled my mom to return and stay with my kids. She came on a one-way ticket, so everything was flexible. My mother-in-law and my dad were waiting on the sidelines to jump in. My family is always supportive, and I have some fantastic in-laws. I'm lucky to have a family that always shows up. I purchased everything I could find online that was suggested for surgery. Wedge pillows, mastectomy pajamas that had pockets for the drains—gross. I bought clothes that I could wear so that I could try and attend my daughter's basketball games, a good old school fanny pack to put my drains in so nobody would see them in public, and lots of other stuff. I wasn't even considering the emotional toll of all of this. It wasn't a thought in my mind yet. I was in mission mode.

Head down, fight face on, and grind.

In the midst of the five-week wait, we tried to bring normalcy to our lives, minus all the surgery supply orders and preparations. We did homework with the kids, signed them up for sports, and attended school stuff. It was time to start searching for a church so we could try to find that faith family. Everywhere we'd been stationed, we had always gone to church, and every community is different. The duty station prior was so mission demanding that we didn't always go, but most Sunday's we were at the chapel on base for church. I reached out to a friend we had been stationed with in Missouri. He and his family had been stationed in Georgia before at the base we were now at, and he'd told me about a church he'd gone to. He sent me the information, and we decided we would try it that Sunday.

At this point, we're four weeks out from surgery. Our first Sunday was great. The music was so good, exactly what I needed, and the sermon was captivating in a way I hadn't heard preaching in a long time. This pastor was GOOD, like—gooooood. The message was straight from the Bible, no fluff. I'm never looking for a "make you feel good" message if it isn't based in truth, and this pastor brought it. In the best way. My husband and I talked about it and decided we'd go back. The next Sunday was even better, and now we're three weeks out from surgery. During the service, another pastor talked about being in "Connect" groups. I could only assume this was akin to the Sunday school classes I had been to most of my life, and "Connect" group was an up-to date way of saying that. We decided that we would stay and try one. It would be good for our kids to have their own Connect groups and meet some other kids, too. We sat in a room with several couples we didn't know and got through our first group study together. The people in the group seemed open, honest, and genuine about their responses, how they lived their lives, and where they struggled. They supported each other, and I thought that was awesome. They had welcomed us in so lovingly and said, "Hey, so we'll see y'all next week and we'll add you to our group chat, etc." It would have been weird to bail out, so we just agreed that we would be back.

Two weeks out from surgery, and we return to the Connect group. Things were about to get awkward. My husband and I discussed it, and I thought, "I'm going to have to tell these people what's about to happen to me because, quite frankly, I think they're going to notice." If chemo becomes part of the plan, they'll definitely take note of me going bald. Can't hide it. So, at the end of class that day, we kind of just dropped the bomb. Surgery was two weeks away, I wasn't 100% sure of the plan following, the diagnosis was new, and we appreciated them welcoming us in.

And no, we didn't need anything. We're military families... we figure it out on our own, remember?

I didn't say it that way obviously (not out loud anyway), but we were quick to put up a wall. I didn't want them to feel pressured; I played it off like we had a plan—it was going to be fine. I live and thrive in the dumpster fire, friends. They just asked if they could pray for us. Sure! That sounds amazing. They placed a chair in the middle of the room and asked if I would sit in it. I sat there, a circle of people around me, all laying a hand on me or my husband, and they prayed for several minutes. That moment forced me to a place where I knew if I was going to come out of this, God had to live in the center of it. The enemy was in full attack mode on my faith, and I knew I had to fight that off. The enemy wasn't about to take me down, not my spirit, not me physically (I hoped), and not my joy.

Hell wasn't going to have me. I'm free. I knew right then that I had to rise every day and make the enemy nervous. He needed to know that I am not the one he's coming for. I hadn't lived my life with the potential that was within to serve God from a deep place of understanding of my own salvation, and the time was now. Those were my thoughts as this group prayed over me. They lit the fire inside me that cannot be put out.

SURGERY DAY WAS HERE!!!!!

Finally, something of substance was taking place instead of taking a pill that made me tired, and I had no idea if it was doing anything. It was an early morning arrival time; 0530, dark outside, cold—even for Florida—it was December. It was calm out. Fall and winter are my favorite seasons, and in the south, winter feels like fall. It brought me serenity to be in cool air, looking at beautiful water. We drove over the river, and I tried to take it all in. My nerves were extra nervy, and in the oddest way, I felt kind of excited. Maybe because I knew it was eviction day, and I would be able to breathe the first breath of relief when I awoke twelve hours from now. I'm not sure, but I allowed myself to feel it. I took it in, knowing that this feeling was one only a cancer patient could experience. I named my tumor Galinda, and it was time for her to make her exit. I know I'm weird to name it. It's fine. You're weird, too, I'm sure, and you know it. Aren't we all kind of weird if we're truthful?

Before we entered the hospital, my husband and I sat in the truck and prayed together. I'd been a Christian since I was young. I hadn't acted like it for a lot of my life, and I regretted all the missed opportunities that came with that, but I couldn't do anything but ask for forgiveness, and know that God is good—all the time. Even in this moment, he was sufficient, and I was forgiven.

Truth be told. It was how I should start every day—in prayer.

We checked in and quietly waited for them to call me back. We didn't talk much. Just sat hand in hand. This type of moment is when choosing your spouse wisely becomes of utmost importance. Spouses can make terrible choices when cancer enters the picture. I've read some horror stories from other breast cancer ladies about how their spouses treated them, cheated on them, and ultimately left them because "they weren't real women anymore" after breast cancer. Absolutely mind-blowing stuff. I was waiting to be called back and just thinking how lucky I was to have such a solid rock of a husband.

We move into the pre-op area to begin getting ready. The hospital chaplain is making rounds and prayed with us in pre-op, then here comes surgeon #1. She goes over the plan, reminds me that lymph nodes are coming out, and that she's going to make the margins around the tumor as clear as possible to ensure the cancer hasn't made its way to my skin. She reassured me that she would seek it all out and remove it. Surgeon # 2 comes in; the fun guy—plastics. Here we are again: me with an open gown, him talking and drawing all over my chest at the same time, and my husband just watching. He finishes up his markings and says, "Okay. Are you ready?" I don't remember saying anything out loud. I just nodded. He said, "Alright, this is going to go well. I'll make it look good. I'll see you in there!" and off he went.

Only a matter of seconds passed, and they came for me. It was game time, put your best face on, and fight time, time to go to war, and Galinda had to die. I was a ball of nerves, and my husband knew it. He hugged me, he kissed me on the forehead, and he said, "I love you; you can do this. You're going to be great. God has this. I'll see you when you wake up." I nodded and said love you as they wheeled me to the O.R.

I was looking down towards my feet, and I saw the O.R. doors ahead. My heart rate was through the roof. I was wondering if I was having a panic attack.

Nahh, I was fine. I'd been fine this whole time.

I don't cry, hardly ever (except when I'm furiously mad, usually), and yet I could feel it coming. I was about to completely lose it. The O.R. doors opened, and I saw a sea of pink scrubs and breast cancer ribbon hair caps. I heard one of the nurses say, "I wore all my pink today since this is a breast cancer case. I see we all had the same idea!" She didn't know I could hear her, but I was so incredibly emotionally humbled in that moment. There and then, I was having a full-on panicked conversation with myself in my head.

This is it, I really have cancer. I'm going to go to sleep and wake up in a totally different body that I don't know. What if I hate it? What if they can't get it all? What if it's everywhere? Get it together. Who even are you right now?

Don't cry. Do. Not. Cry!

I could no longer pretend like it wasn't real, and I could no longer hide from thoughts and emotions. They were consuming me. They rolled my bed next to the operating table and told me to start sliding over.

That was it, y'all.

I hit that operating table and lost it. My face must have shown it, and I started to cry, and not just cry, but sob, while in my head I was still telling myself to get it together. One of the nurses grabbed my hand, held it, and rubbed my arm. She said, "We're going to take our time. We're going to get you ready, and you can have a minute. It's going to be okay. I know this is scary, but we got you, hun." Her words brought me off the ledge; she took some deep breaths with me, and the anesthesiologists came in, both named Chris. The Chris's said, "You know what, we're just going to give you a little fun cocktail we like to make that will help relax you. We won't go to sleep until you're ready, but we'll get the party going." They were funny and calming as most anesthesiologists are, I've found. I calmed down, got my bearings back after a couple of minutes, and then one of the Chris's said, "How are you feeling? Do you think you're ready?"

I took a deep breath in and exhaled slowly, "Let's do this."

Ten hours pass. I'm slowly coming to my senses and can tell I'm in a bed being rolled into a room. I'm in the PACU recovery unit. I can't open my eyes yet, I can't speak, but I can hear. The very first words I hear are from the nurse pushing my bed, and she's talking to the nurse at the foot of my bed. She said,

"Booooy, that was a God thing, wasn't it?" to which he replied,

"It sure was!"

I have no idea what they were talking about, but I'll never forget those words. A nod from the Lord that he was there. There would be two nights in the hospital before I could go home. The breast surgeon visited me the following morning and told me that she was able to get it all with negative margins, meaning there was no residual cancer around the edges. She told me that it was closer to my sternum than she expected (1mm from touching), so she had scraped extra skin from the area to make sure, and she said she had to dig deeper for my lymph nodes than she planned, so I was probably going to be extra sore in that armpit. She sent all the tissue and nodes to pathology, and would have my pathology report in a couple of days to call me with. The plastic surgeon followed and said everything went well. He was happy with how everything looked. He gave me tons of instructions on wound care, etc., and said a nurse would be around to show us how to use the drains (gross). I would follow up in the office with them both in a week. The drive home consisted of sleeping mixed with brief conversations of relief with my husband.

We had made it through the first phase of treatment!

Two days after I got home, I got a call from the breast surgeon.

My pathology report was in.

Even though my PET scan was clear, I did have a small tumor in one of the three lymph nodes she removed. It hadn't moved outside of that one node yet, thankfully, but now the thoughts of chemotherapy began to creep to the front of my mind. She said my chain of lymph nodes that are behind my collar bone and sternum, she doesn't remove, so for sure there would need to be radiation to make sure all of those are reached. Radiation is always the final step of treatment, so that could be months away. I would discuss the path report again in the office with her and my oncologist the following week to set the plan.

That call calmed me because 'ol Galinda was gone, but it created new worry. I was trying my hardest NOT to worry. The oncologist told me she wanted me to be as low stress as possible—for the rest of my life. Stress creates all kinds of problems, including displaying itself in physical ailments like cancer. That part makes me chuckle. Because I'm stressed about trying not to be stressed.

That's anxiety, I guess.

The follow-up appointments were soon underway; my husband was there, and ready with pen in hand and the binder out. I got through the surgical follow-up, and they said I look great. I'm a "good healer."

Wheeellll, thank you.

"My body knows to get itself together", I thought. I may have been a little prideful, but my body had just gone through a double mastectomy. A double amputation, and she was coming out on the other side like a champ!

The oncologist came in, and I could feel that things were about to get heavy. The air in the room was almost palpable; it felt so thick to me. She was holding lots of papers. A nurse joined her, and she walked in quickly. I could tell we have a lot to get through.

"Okay. Here we go." She says with a comforting smile on her face, letting my spirit settle. She has a knack for that, and it's a beautiful thing. She covered the pathology report and told me that she doesn't yet have the DNA information she ordered from the tumor, but she's confident that doing chemotherapy will be the right decision and that when she finally gets the DNA report, it will corroborate her decision.

She asked me to trust her judgment on this because she felt that this was the right thing to do to save my life and give me longevity. She said, "We have to start soon. I want you to begin chemo as soon as you reach four weeks post-op, and I'd like you to get a port placed before that. It's another procedure, but you will only be partially sedated. They will place your port on the right side of your chest." She went on to explain how the port works, why its location is important, and how it will be accessed for treatment each time.

Instantly, I could feel my heart beating fast and hard. I looked at my watch and saw my heart rate slowly rise as she talked. I was ill-prepared, maybe living a little in denial until this moment, just trying to will it into existence so that I wouldn't have to do this. I had long, straight, beautiful brownish-blond hair that I loved. It was one of the things that I thought was most beautiful about me. Lots of women struggle with their appearance, and I'm one of them. My husband loves me no matter what, and God bless him for that, but my hair made me feel pretty. People often commented on my hair, my whole life they had, and in this moment, as petty as it sounds, I was panicking inside thinking about it all falling out. I was only one week out from a massive surgery with more than a hundred sutures, and now I have to have another small procedure for port placement in just a couple of weeks so that I'm prepared to start chemo.

Did I trust the oncologist was good enough to know that I was going to need chemo? What if the DNA came back, and I could have opted out?

You can bet your paycheck I knew she was good enough. My oncologist is my hype-woman, my steady hand on the shaky bridge, and so incredibly educated and intellectual. She's not just smart because it's her job. She has genuine care, drive, and goals for her patients to survive and thrive. She doesn't talk fluff; she gives direct advice, and she has told me repeatedly that everything she wants me to do is because it will save my life and help me live much longer.

You may be wondering about me questioning myself about potentially opting out of chemo if it were an option. I'm glad you asked. No, I wouldn't have opted out. I wasn't here to take chances or just hope a different diet would save me. I was 38 years old. I had two kids, and unless the Lord called me home on his own accord, I had ZERO plan of accepting anything except complete full-scale Victory. This was war, and I wasn't leaving this earth because I chose to opt out.

I CAME TO FIGHT. MAKE NO MISTAKE.

For maybe the first time in my life, I was legitimately afraid, though. I had known people with cancer. I once had a supervisor who had fought cancer three times and done chemo. I'd learned from him what it was like, but never really understood. You know by now I don't do emotions. I'm not a fan. If I'm crying, just know that I'm past angry. I'm a rage crier, and I'm trying not to start swinging. I don't necessarily think that's the right way to deal with emotions, but it's who I am, nonetheless. I like to laugh all the time. I'll die a wrinkly-faced old woman because I laughed so much, and I'm down for that all day! I don't like drama. I want joy!

But fear? I was afraid in a new way. I'm sure my husband was afraid, but he wouldn't tell me, not at the time anyway, and I'm glad he didn't. He sat through that appointment, took notes, and all the paperwork she gave me. His face never changed. Stoic is the best word I can use for him. He looked calm, collected, level-headed, and unafraid at that moment. It's what I needed. We couldn't both fall apart.

The chemo options were presented. I was shocked that there were options, but they came with different drugs to be used and different time frames. I had to let her know that day or the next which option I wanted to do. It was SO overwhelming I couldn't decide. She ordered my port placement and said they would call me soon with the date. I asked if I could think about chemo and let her know. I thought she would just say, "Suuure; send me a message when you decide," except I heard, "You can think about it today, but I have to know by tomorrow morning." The pressure was immense. One option would mean traveling every week for sixteen weeks, and there was a high risk of allergic reactions in addition to the chance of my white blood cell count being too low to administer treatment. The other option was better for my husband. I was still trying to maintain some consistency at home for him as well as the kids. I would only do an infusion every twenty-one days. It would take longer, about eighteen weeks, but the risk of adverse reaction up front was lower. I would be given a fancy patch on my arm on the day of my infusion. The day after, it would auto-inject, and the medication goal was to pump up my white blood cell production so I could stay on track with infusions.

We left her office and made it to the first-floor lobby. There are many areas to sit and a nice garden in the center, so that people can have some quiet time. I got to a table before I started to tear up. It was so much pressure, and all I could think of was what if I chose the wrong one and I die because it didn't work. My husband sat down with me, had me box breathe slowly (funny cause I had previously taught his airmen how to box breathe under pressure—look it up, it's great for stress), and when I was ready to talk, we got the paper out and went over it.

A lady who was working an event where survivors were celebrated came over to the table, handed me a small box of tissues, and went back to her event. Another God wink that I was in the right place. We talked through options, travel, planning for the kids, and several other things for about twenty minutes. Ultimately, I decided before we left the hospital. Option Two would be my path. I called upstairs to oncology and let them know. We retreated to the parking garage to begin the journey home again, feeling somewhat defeated this time.

Halfway home, I started getting notifications that appointments were being loaded into "My Chart," which was the hospital's online portal. I logged in to see what the deal was. There it was. My port placement was already scheduled for two weeks from that day, and then I saw the big one. My first infusion was scheduled for ten days after my port placement, and it would fall one day after my four-week follow-up from surgery.

# 8

## WHEN MY HAIR FELL OUT, MY SPIRIT DIDN'T

*"Never be afraid to trust an unknown future to a known God."*

- Corrie Ten Boom

I knew this was going to suck. I wasn't even going to be healed from the major surgery before I would start with the poison that would save my life, AKA chemotherapy. The surgeon had prepared me for an eight to twelve-week recovery. I would be getting the drains removed the day before my first infusion.

This was going to HURT.

I knew that the mental pain would be difficult. I'm a strong-willed, stubborn, do-it-myself, high pain tolerance kind of gal, but this was new pain. The physical pain was going to be bad, and I didn't know yet to what level of bad. I hated throwing up more than anything in the world and would fight nausea, but I knew it was coming, and it was just time to get used to it. I had two weeks to mentally prepare, but there is no way to prepare for chemo. It's the unknown, and I was doing it while only a third of the way through the surgical healing. I was really feeling the sense of urgency with treatment now. I was in deep; this was my life now. I was a cancer patient, not my normal self, and I knew that my personality was about to be under attack from a bunch of drugs I needed to have if I wanted to stay above the ground and not below it.

*I have learned over the years that when one's mind is made up, this diminishes fear; knowing what must be done does away with fear.*

- Rosa Parks

It had to be done, so I busted out my big girl undies, had many pep talks with myself, and most importantly, I prayed. The fight I knew I was in had only just begun, and I had no idea how things were about to go. It was like being in an MMA fight, but with no training, I didn't know the bell was ringing, how many rounds there would be, or what my opponent was capable of. I only had the words of others and guesses. The list of side effects is crazy, people. It's crazy. I learned that in the first four days following an infusion, I would experience a set of side effects, and as they began to subside on day four, another round of different side effects would set in from days four to seven. That became the flow of every infusion.

My port was placed, and it wasn't too bad, but now I was ten days from the start of it. Infusion day requires three appointments. I had to arrive very early, have a blood draw, then see oncology so they could clear my blood panel. Only then could I go to the infusion floor to be weighed and wait for the pharmacist to mix the drugs and give the green light. The actual infusion took about three hours. It's several different bags of meds, including nausea medication (YAY!) and steroids. On day one, the day of infusion, I felt weird, but overall, pretty good. I would clean the house, do dishes, and try to hangout with my kids. Day two would start to go downhill rapidly, and days three through five were awful.

I have to preface the rest of this chapter by telling you that "chemo brain" or "brain fog" is very real. Many things were altered, including my ability to use vocabulary in the way I could before, my eyesight, and my ability to think clearly enough to make complete thoughts. I often, even now, because it doesn't ever fully resolve, lose a word or phrase in the middle of a sentence. It may be acronyms I've used my whole life or just basic descriptive words. I know that I am the visual representation of the little circle spinny thing on a website when the page is loading. That's exactly what's happening in my brain at the moment.

I just look like I'm buffering. I'll eventually get it, remember it, or circle back to the thought, but it takes me a minute sometimes. Makes it kind of hard to write a book, but I'm doing my best.

The posts below will cover a lot of time throughout this journey. My plan was never to journal my experience through social media, but it became a way to share how I was experiencing the journey that is cancer. I very rarely posted on social media before the diagnosis. My life was quickly changing, but my spirit was growing in strength. I chose a single social media post for each major event from diagnosis to survivorship. Secondarily, this kept me from having to explain myself eighty times over via text and email when people had questions. During chemo, I was exhausted to the point where I didn't look at my phone for days. I didn't answer when it rang unless it was the hospital. I didn't respond to texts, even from my own mom, until a day or two later. By making posts, I was curious to see a potential positive side effect where others could see my fight, and maybe it would help someone else struggling.

I do not and will not ever engage in arguing, debating, or bullying online, so my posts were intended to invoke positivity, maybe thought-provoking questions or comments, and most importantly, I wanted to inspire someone else to keep going, even when the days are hard. These posts were my milestones.

Was there awful stuff happening in between them and in the background?

ABSOLUTELY!

But I don't live in the background, and I will not settle for or sit in misery. I can't. I will hold my head high, I will stand when it hurts to stand, and I will move forward. And on the days that it brought me to my knees, I prayed more than usual. There were plenty of times I lay in bed or on the couch and listened to worship music. I couldn't always attend church or even leave my bed, but I was holding church in my heart and mind. Through music and prayer, I would press on because that's who God created me to be. He gave me a "take one on the chin and ask for another" kind of spirit and personality.

Beneath each post, there's some context or explanation of the bad and the ugly that also took place following that post. Don't forget the chemo posts I made during the infusion. It was the day I felt the best through the whole process, so my mind was more right on infusion day than it would be for the twenty days following it each time.

In its entirety, here we go...

*October 11: First cancer post after the PCS.*
*My notification to my world of friends.*

**Natalie McCoy**
October 11, 2023 · 🎗

Today begins the 2nd part of this PCS to GA; the unexpected part. The day after we arrived, I found out I have Breast Cancer so today I begin the journey to healthy at MD Anderson in FL. Make no mistake- I come to win. This hospital is going to make the fight much easier. I believe in the power of prayer so if you find the time in your day to add me to your prayers I appreciate it! Pray for Israel while you're there. 2 Timothy 4:7- I have fought the good fight. I have finished the race. I have kept the faith.

❤👍😊 220                                                      137 comments

*December 5: Double Mastectomy (DMX) Day*

**Natalie McCoy**
December 5, 2023 · 🎗

TODAY IS SURGERY DAY! Step 2 in the long goodbye to cancer! Sometimes mountains are in our paths & we simply have to climb. To all our family helping us out- THANK YOU! To all those who sent cards and packages- you're appreciated! And to my MILITARY FAMILY/CLUB LANGLEY- y'all have been with me since midnight of day 1 and you continue to show up because you're true ride or die's and I'm forever thankful for each of you. Lastly, to those who went before me in this fight & those still fighting- you ARE inspiration and let's kick ass! God is good, all the time. See y'all in a few days.

❤👍😊 216                                                      75 comments

I referred to Club Langley in this post, amongst many others. They're all important. What I didn't know was that in a separate Club Langley chat, the ladies were creating a calendar and rotation (coordinated by the teacher in the group, of course, we'll call her Stanford!), and that rotation was them signing up to send me a care package each month. They went through this rotation twice, I think. We all PCS'd and were spread far and wide. I began getting packages from all over the world, Korea, England, Germany, North Dakota, California, and Texas. It was incredible. It took me a few months to figure out what was happening, and when I finally questioned Josey, she spilled the tea:

"Yeah, we all decided we want to send you stuff, so Stanford set us up in a rotation so that you would get something from one of the families each month."

My military FRAMILY had come through again. The PCS season separated us all, but only by location. There were trips to see each other already planned, and Pop Pop was stopping in Georgia on a TDY soon and would get to stay with us. These are the military spouse friends you're looking for, y'all! The ones that show up, in their sweatpants or from another state, just so you feel loved. Don't settle for less!

The day before my first chemo infusion, the Club Langley chat pinged, and it said, "This is for you!" It was a two and a half-minute video that they had all put together of each of the families sending me prayers, their thoughts, and encouragement for what was coming the next day. It was so heartfelt, thoughtful, and precisely what I needed. I teared up and watched over and over. I saved it, and I watch it from time to time when things get hard.

*January 11: Chemo #1*

**Natalie McCoy**
January 11, 2024 ·

Perseverance: Persistence in doing something despite difficulty or delay in achieving success.

This IS 2024: to persevere & ultimately overcome.

Today is chemo treatment #1 & it's the part I didn't know I was most anxious about until it was real. Surgery went phenomenal with the best TEAM of surgeons/oncologists one could ask for. I heal well so I was nervous but not yet bald & sick. This is the hard part y'all. I'm thankful for those of you that are my consistent prayer warriors & cheerleaders- trust me; I feel it! The outpouring of love has truly been remarkable. To my 3 cancer warriors who've been in this terrible fight—your words are irreplaceable so thank you for being on this journey with me.

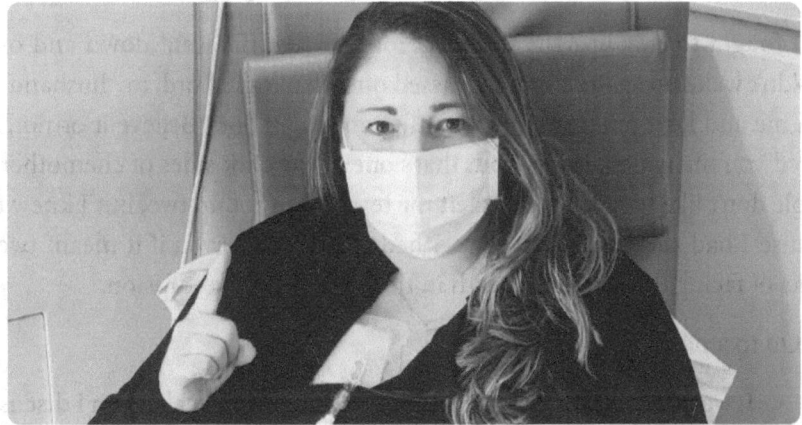

❤️👍😢 252                                        98 comments   1 share

Lots to unpack here; stay with me!

The first chemo treatment was the scariest, most intense single experience of my entire life.

There is nothing to prepare you for what happens to your body after the first infusion. To complicate my physical response to this infusion, I was five weeks post-MAJOR surgery, and I believe that's what put me over the edge.

The night of day two post-infusion will never leave my memory fully. I have processed it through trauma therapy, but it will never leave me. I awoke in the middle of the night, lying on my back with my surgical pillows around me. I was drenched in sweat and experiencing my first raging hot flash; I needed to vomit, and I couldn't get up. My whole body wouldn't move, and every joint was in immense pain; even my fingers hurt. The spot where Galinda once lived felt sunken in and like someone was pressing in on it. I was too weak to move my limbs, couldn't get the covers off me, or move the pillows. I was freaking out because I was losing control of my bodily functions. I was crying, and it hurt to breathe. I flung one arm and managed to hit my husband, who literally went from lying down to standing on my side of the bed in a matter of a few seconds. He could see the terror. He picked me up from the bed and held me up while I tried to shuffle my feet. I was trying to get to the toilet to vomit gracefully, but I was so dizzy. We made it to the bathroom, and I began to lose the fight with consciousness. My thoughts were racing as the tunnel vision of losing consciousness closed in. My vision was going dark, and I was thinking,

"This is what it feels like to die. I'm literally dying right now."

I fought to stay upright and alert for fear that if I went down and out, I wouldn't wake up again. Boom! I passed out. Thank the Lord, my husband was with me and kept me from face-planting on a tile floor. Believe it or not, I've spared you many details here, but that's one of the dark sides of chemotherapy people don't like to talk about. It left me terrified of round two, but I knew that because I had survived round one, I had to continue, even if it meant twenty weeks of facing the feeling of death in the days following infusion.

On to a positive note!

It wasn't just Club Langley who showed up big. Recall when I discussed the Connect group that surrounded me in prayer when I told them what was about to happen. These people have become the biblical community that every

Christian on the planet should strive to be for others and should hope to be a part of. They live out what it looks like to be a Christian. Being Christian is a VERB, not a noun. It is not a description of a group of people who are better than others, putting on suits and dresses on Sunday, going to church to be reminded that they are better than others, and don't deserve judgment.

Ohhhh, no!

Christians are to set out in life on mission to be the hands and feet of Jesus. They should demonstrate what love is to others with action, not just words, and this Connect group did just that. Without asking for a thing (because they knew we wouldn't), they began arriving at my house with meals on a schedule. They stopped by to pray over me and see what I needed. One of them finally told me, "you might as well send me your chemo dates because we aren't going to stop."

I have to remind y'all—They DON'T KNOW ME. They don't know my background, they don't know that I just spent four years struggling to find a church home. They don't know that my biggest struggle in life is my MOUTH and the words that leave it. They don't know me. And it didn't matter. They showed up anyway because they are full of love.

*January 26: My sister-in-law is visiting. It becomes*
*obvious my hair has to be addressed soon.*

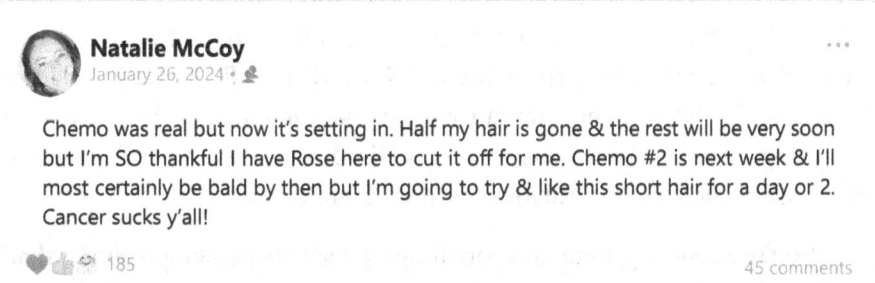

**Natalie McCoy**
January 26, 2024 · 🎗

Chemo was real but now it's setting in. Half my hair is gone & the rest will be very soon but I'm SO thankful I have Rose here to cut it off for me. Chemo #2 is next week & I'll most certainly be bald by then but I'm going to try & like this short hair for a day or 2. Cancer sucks y'all!

❤️👍🥰 185                                                   45 comments

This is the day it all sank in. I love my sister-in-law so much that I trusted her to pick up scissors and cut my hair short. She'd never done that before, but it didn't matter. My hair was falling out in large handfuls, and it was painful, not just mentally. It physically hurt as it was falling out. My scalp felt bruised everywhere. The nurses told me it was coming. I just blocked out that conversation until this day.

Let me take a moment to provide some knowledge that some folks need to hear. One of the WORST things you can say to a cancer patient is, "It's just hair. It'll grow back." Those hit me like fighting words. Do people really think that I don't know it's "just hair?" I'm fully aware of what it is. It's part of my identity, it's what I thought made me beautiful; it was long and straight, and it was what God had adorned my head with. One of the hardest things I've ever gone through was my hair falling out. So keep those comments in your head, cause you'll never understand unless it's you.

On that note, saying things like, "Well, I read that if you're going to get cancer, this is the kind to get," to any cancer patient is not acceptable. This isn't said to breast cancer patients as often, but I have a thyroid cancer buddy, someone said that to. I'd be ready to throw hands in a parking lot if that was uttered to me. Some people have ALL the AUDACITY.

Think before you talk, folks. As always, WORDS MATTER.

If you can't be supportive without offering what you think may be comforting to hear, just don't talk. Standing next to me or hugging me was more than enough. I didn't need everyone sending me diet plans, workout plans, oils and supplements, or lifestyle additions that their cousins' sisters' friend used for her cancer, and it magically is going away. Those things cannot compete with what we KNOW in modern medicine works. I am young. I want to live, and I have a husband and kids who need me, and I need them. How could I ever look my girls in the face and tell them I'm sorry I'm in hospice and going to die early because I wanted to try everything holistic instead of trusting my oncologists to do what they specialize in? How? There is FOR SURE a place in this journey for holistic and alternative medicine, and I'll write about that later, but during the initial treatment phase. It's all-out war, and I went full-send to ensure my chances of survival long-term were maxed out.

If you're a cancer patient and you disagree with the paragraph above, that's OK. We all get different treatments, make our own choices about what we do on this journey, and the choice is solely yours. I support that wholeheartedly, whether I agree with it or not. The words above are my thoughts for regular people, in the hope of building some understanding of how to communicate with cancer patients.

The next day: It's my daughter's birthday.

I didn't make a post on this day, but it is the day my husband had to sit in our bathroom and shave my head. I only made it one day with short hair before so much fell out that it had to go. One of my girls had a basketball game. An hour before we had to leave for the game, I decided it was time. I had delayed it as long as I could. I couldn't go to the game with huge bald spots, but I wanted to be there for my daughter. My thoughts were all over the place. Rose was still visiting, so that helped my girls with additional support, but I cried sitting in the bathroom as what was left of my beautiful hair (and part of my identity) fell to the floor. It felt like watching my personality fall away in pieces, and I wondered if I would ever get it back. That was it, I was bald. I had a scarf I'd bought but never taken out of the package. I quickly got it out to learn how to tie it and to try to cover my head so my kids wouldn't be embarrassed. My girls were so supportive, but they're kids. I knew it was going to embarrass them even if they didn't act that way. They didn't want to have to explain it to their friends or talk about it, and I didn't want them to have to. I got the scarf on my head, and to the game we went. I tried so hard to be normal.

Something I regret about this day didn't even occur to me until one year later. My youngest daughter came to me as I got ready for her birthday party and said, "Hey, Mom. I'm really happy that we get to celebrate this year. Last year, I was just so sad because you had to shave your head on my birthday." The girl stopped me in my tracks. How had I not remembered that it happened on her birthday?!

Now I make sure that I really pay attention to details like that and how it impacted my kids.

*February 1: Chemo #2 / My 39th birthday is approaching quickly!*

**Natalie McCoy**
February 1, 2024 ·

Chemo round 2 of 6 has begun!

"Don't Let the Enemy Steal Your Joy"

Today—I can't lie & say I'm not anxious for the days following this treatment cause the first one was ROUGH....but. The enemy won't steal my joy because I control that! So—with that said—

I'm going to mention some things that bring me joy & I'd
LOVE TO HEAR WHAT BRINGS YOU JOY TODAY 😊

1. My husband is the best caregiver, husband, father, leader, etc. I could have ever imagined. I could not do this without him.

2. My family is the best. My mom, dad & in-laws have all rotated & continue to do so to help us take care of our kids.

3. My friends are 2nd to none. Y'all show up on the regular–some of you...literally–show up here in Georgia & that's awesome.

4. My next-door neighbors are fantastic, have become friends & are helping us keep the kids lives going.

5. Speaking of kids–I got 2 ballers on the basketball court keeping my heart rate up at games (if you haven't watched a 5th grade girls game....whew–take your BP meds before)

6. My kids basketball teams' parents showed up! They help us a ton!

7. Our church is in it to win it with us & that's unbeatable

8. My cancer buddy, (the Prankster) is in the fight with me & while this sucks. It's something else's ass we can kick together

9. My military family is close, far & worldwide but I talk to or see 1 of you daily. That's what military family does & y'all dont disappoint. You show up. Every single time.

10. My homie, "Vegas" (for the purpose of this book) is retiring today & bringing his family to good 'ol Georgia!! See you soon homie!

Happy Thursday–let's see some joy in these comments!

❤️👍😊 207                                                                 65 comments

I was so happy at the end of this post, and I want to share some of the comments I got back. They made me laugh, smile, and have joy. It's exactly what I was going for when I wrote the post. Here are some of the comments I received:

*We celebrated my nephew turning seventeen yesterday. Last weekend, I ice fished for the first time. Didn't catch a dang thing, but had a great time! Looking forward to a weekend in Denver starting tomorrow with my guy.*

*My family brings me incredible joy too! I also have wonderful friends and an amazing church family.*

*Thanking the Lord for this beautiful day.*

*My joy is reading this and trying to follow along. We are all broken in some way but relying on God has also served me well and it sounds like you are also in a good place with your faith.*

*My joy my fur kids and family both there to love unconditional.*

*What brings me joy today??? Seeing you smile through this, That I got a cookie sandwich (snickerdoodles with 1/2 inch vanilla butter cream between them), that tomorrow is my 51st birthday, that my brothers chemo is coming to an end... so much joy today!*

*My family brings me joy!! We are so lucky to have each other! (from my mother-in-law)*

*Love this!! No one can steal your joy!! My family and friends bring me joy daily! Also, I love your scarf!! You need to show me how you tied it! (from one of my cancer buddies)*

*My joy today is having friends like you who are strong and bad ass!*

*My joy is that my family is always there for me*

*I enjoy reading your updates. You are very strong person and I know with all family and friends you will get through this. I know God is always with you. Prayers are continuing throughout this process for you and your family*

*I get so much joy from helping you and others. Love your Barbie pink! (from my mom)*

*My joy is seeing your strong Faith through this journey.*

*You and your courage bring me joy.*

*What brings me joy today....seeing you smile and knowing you are around people who are there for you!*

*\*\*\*\*\*Love your attitude! Except when you're sassy and push coworkers to the ground. But really I need to be more like you. (This comment is from the one I call The Prankster, as you can see there's a story about a "scuffle" we had at work : ) )*

*Your dad brings me joy! Seeing how he loves you and your husband is amazing. Seeing him totally get crazy at a 5th grade BBall game is the BEST. we're with you all the way! More HEB treats headed to GA. (If you aren't familiar with HEB..get familiar. It's a Texas thang. This is from my step-mom)*

*Love you girl. You got this. You are stronger than you know. Keep holding onto joy.*

*Love ya Kiddo! You're my Hero! (from my dad)*

---

*February 22: Chemo #3. I turned 39 between infusions two and three. Not at all how I thought I'd have a birthday, but it made me look at age 40 with wonder and awe.*

**Natalie McCoy**
February 22, 2024 · 👤

CHEMO #3 OF 6-TODAY IS HALFWAY Y'ALL, YEE & HAW! 🤠

Before yesterday's appointments, we went for a walk around the bay & 1 the pics. here got into my thoughts.

🌴 The Palm Tree: a little palm, under a concrete overpass, living close to water but not directly by it, covered from most of the sunlight & rain, hidden from nature, yet ALIVE & THRIVING in the face of resistance.

I want to be this palm 🌴. Those that know me well & have worked with me have described me as stubborn, direct, assertive, caring, the "sheriff", people loving, and a few other things, lol. And those are all correct but what I feel deep in my soul came from this tree & it was:

‼️ BE RELENTLESS IN THE PURSUIT OF LIVING ‼️ Be who you are & be it well cause if we are going to live we need to make it count. FEAR 🌴 HAS 🌴 NO 🌴 PLACE 🌴 HERE . Isaiah 41 has a lot to offer on this but Fear Not, friends—he is with us!

I have close friends fighting this cancer fight alongside me & I can't stand that but we will Be Relentless & we will keep showing up!

Wake Up, Be Bold & Repeat

❤️👍😊 173                                    38 comments

This was the halfway point. Number three was in progress. Each infusion, I sat quietly and listened to people ring the bell. The first time, I cried because it didn't feel as if I'd ever reach the bell, even though I walked by it to and from the infusion pod where I received treatment. This round, there were four or five people who won! They got to ring the bell, and it was getting closer to my time. Everyone on the floor claps and cheers when that bell rings because when one of us wins, WE ALL WIN! That palm tree remained in my mind, and I see it as a symbol of the pursuit of a fruitful life now.

I referred to Isaiah 41 in this post. Matter of fact, Isaiah 41:10 is tattooed on my wrist as a constant reminder that fear cannot live in my soul because I'm forgiven and I have salvation. Even if I die, I know where I'll be.

*Isaiah 41:10: Fear not, for I am with you; Be not dismayed,*
*for I am your God. I will strengthen you; I will help you,*
*I will uphold you with My righteous right hand.*

---

*March 14: Chemo #4*

**Natalie McCoy**
March 14, 2024 · 👤

CHEMO #4 OF 6:

"This is no time for ease and comfort. It is time to dare and endure." Winston Churchill

Some say it's the "downhill phase" & it's exciting. While it is, for chemo (& i am excited) there is much more to follow after & ill go 1 day, 1 step at a time until I ring the bell! 🌴 So.....that leads me to where I sit today: In the GRIND. Recovery between rounds is becoming harder & taking longer so I put my head down & press because that's who I've been taught (by many great people) to be.

Diamonds are created with pressure so I'm trying to come out of this shiny & durable.

💌Thank ALL Y'ALL for the messages, texts, calls, cards, prayers & thoughts. SOOO many of reached out that I've lost count but I haven't forgotten your words. They've all come at the right time whether you knew it or not.

👊 Let's throw hands #4! Grind & Press Relentlessly. 🙏God is Good, All the Time!

 210

56 comments

I was so fatigued. Side effects were wearing me down. It was an endless list of problems you never considered, and you just wanted to hide and get rid of them. People don't understand and oftentimes don't want to see or hear it. They live in happy bubbles; eternal optimists, some of them call themselves, but many of them just like to keep it out of sight, out of mind. Now, I have friends who are eternal optimists, and I love them dearly. Not all folks that have this kind of spirit want to be oblivious, so don't hear what I'm NOT saying.

Some people prefer to be oblivious to the things in life that aren't pretty, cause discomfort for others or themselves, and that includes talking to or being too close to a cancer patient. People would ask me, "How are you? How's treatment?" and I had to decide if I was going to really answer them or just say, "It's going good," because I knew they didn't really want to know. They knew they were supposed to ask and then act like it mattered to them. In reality, it didn't matter much to anyone except my caregiver husband. He was in this fight with me, in all its ugliness. He has seen me in rare form; he's seen me in ball gowns with my hair done, thin and beautiful. Now he's seen me, bald, no eyebrows or eyelashes, bloated, full of side effects, and looking like death, and he always showed up and loved me. He continuously reminds me that he said, "in sickness and in health." Ugggh, what a guy!

Back to my quick soap box: I didn't need it to matter to others, and that's truthful. I had only wished that they would stop asking. If you don't want to know the ugly truths that are cancer, don't ask the patient. Cause we know we make you uncomfortable, and it's an energy drain to us to amuse you by answering to make YOU feel better that we said we're fine. WE ARE NOT FINE, but you don't have to pretend to want to know if you don't really want to know. I'm a truth teller…I'll tell you everything. I'm an open book (ahheem… exhibit A) and I have nothing to hide. There were times (because I'm me) that I intentionally told people more than I knew they wanted to hear just to make them squirm. I could see how uncomfortable I made them, and I did it anyway. I thrive in uncomfortable situations because I believe discomfort is where growth is obtained, so it wasn't nice of me to do that, but I did.

It drove me crazy when I would get comments from people saying," praying for you", or just the little emoji to say the same. It drove me crazy because a lot of times I got those comments from people I knew weren't actually praying for me. I didn't think they prayed to begin with. That was how I felt. I received many supportive comments from people I knew were praying and thinking of me, and whether they actually did it or not mattered little. It was the fact that they were taking time to type the comment that I should have been appreciative of.

Looking back provides perspective, and I was angry, exhausted, and didn't trust people's authenticity in talking to me. I'm not saying that I'm right, just saying that was my reality.

*April 4: Chemo #5*

**Natalie McCoy**
April 4, 2024 · 🔒

Chemo #5: Kickin' cancer w/chemo ninjas!

Today, I'm fatigued, worn down & the chemo side effects have really become constant. My body feels like it's legit in a fight, throwin' hands every day. 🤼

But- let me tell you about my Spirit: I'm here for Jesus ✝️, my family 👨‍👩‍👧, my friends, sports 🏒 ....and eventually a drink to accompany my tacos. My SPIRIT is not afraid & is in the fight!

If you know me well, you know that sports get in my soul big time & I am FIRED UP about some sports right now. Women's basketball 🏀 is trailblazing & I can't wait for the Final Four. My Texas Rangers ⚾ came out opening week swinging like we're back to take it again & the Olympics 🎌 is coming! I needed the extra boost of pure competition & athletic talent to get me alive and excited!! Go find what lights your fire friends: sports, camping, lakes, oceans, whatever....it's not in your phone though, its outside, really living! 😊

Lastly, the song playing in my head & keeping the balance is "You Already Won" by Shane & Shane It's like my personal fight song. Take a listen if you haven't before. SEE Y'ALL IN 21 DAYS TO RING THIS BELL BABAY!

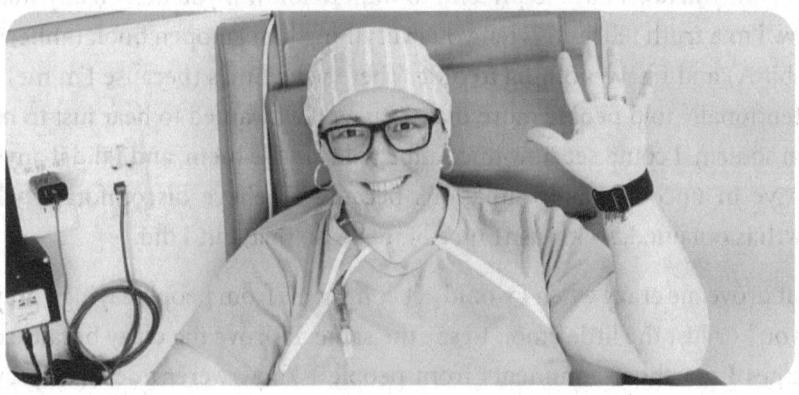

❤️👍😆 188                                        58 comments

I was ON ONE this round because I knew I was one away. Just one more and I could be done. There was a fire burning in my soul that missed the activity of daily normal life and all that comes with that. In my head, I would soon be normal again. HAHAHAHA....all the cancer patients are laughing right now. There is no normal again, only a new normal.

My soul was also changing and turning back to God. The Sundays that I was in church, I couldn't get through the music without crying. The words were like God was speaking directly to me every time. It was what I needed to hear at the perfect time. The song I mentioned in the post became a sticking point for me, and that song would shape part of my future, which I hadn't ever considered.

*April 25: Chemo #6 of 6: BELL  RINGING DAY! (Post #1 of 2)*

**Natalie McCoy**
April 25, 2024 ·

It's Game Day Baby! I have much more left in my journey BUT TODAY, I'm at the summit of the hardest mountain I've ever climbed & starting my descent! This, by far has been the hardest 20 weeks of my life & today I get to complete this step of the journey .

"Difficult roads often lead to beautiful destinations ." Zig Ziglar

I don't yet know WHAT I'm supposed to do with this journey but I know something in my future will make it make sense . God has a plan & I'm here for it. I hope whatever it may be allows me to bless others in the ways I've been blessed the last 8 months.

Isaiah 41:10 : fear not, for I am with you; be not dismayed, for I am your God; I will strengthen you, I will help you, I will uphold you with my righteous right hand.

This verse has been my go to for a decade in times of difficulty because it reminds me that even though I may feel alone sometimes; I'm not.

I'm SO proud of my kids for their resilient attitudes through all this & I could NOT have made it through this without the best husband & caregiver ever. He may have that mean face but he's made of gold & diamonds y'all.

I'll be back in 3ish hours with the bell!

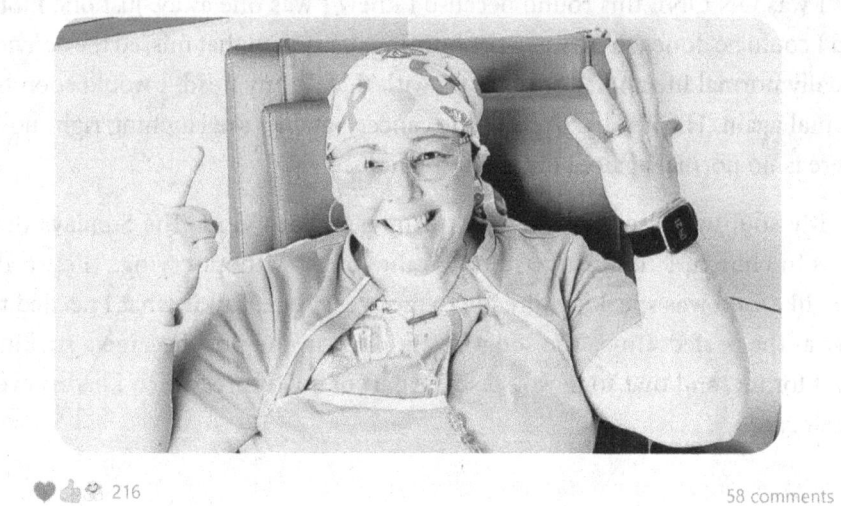

 216                                        58 comments

*...Three hours later...*
*Post #2 with video of me RINGING THE BELL!!!!*

**Natalie McCoy**
April 25, 2024 · 🏃

This part is OVER!!!!!! I MADE IT FRIENDS! To anyone still in this fight...keep going, don't stop, don't look back! Go get it.

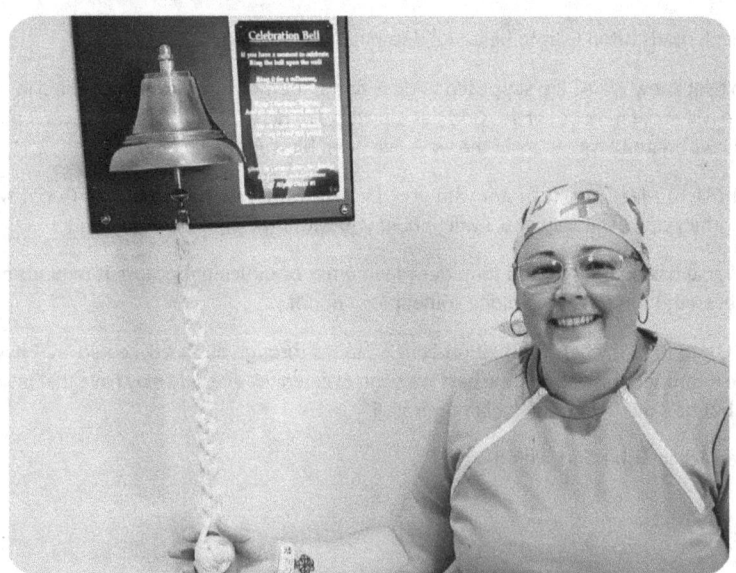

💜 👍 🌸 257                                    67 comments

When revisiting my first post of this day, I get chills. I said that I didn't know what I should do with this journey, but that God had a plan for me. Well, guess what the plan entails?

A Book.

Y'all, I don't even like to read.

This round was heavy with side effects, and I was more exhausted than I thought was possible. For the first time, I didn't leave my bed for three days. I only got up to use the bathroom. I had crackers and a water bottle, and I slept on and off for three straight days.

Previously, I at least got up in the morning and moved to the couch for the day. This was different. Day four was rough, but remember, the side effects start to shift on day four. I decided I had to make myself get up and shower. That's right—I didn't shower for three days either. It was too much. But on day four, I showered, and I made myself a big glass of sweet tea. After round three, I learned that sweet tea on day four or five had the potential to change my life. I mean, it was like life juice. I'm from the south—sweet tea is important. Chemo had messed up my taste so badly that I was afraid to eat certain things. The nurses told me early on not to eat foods I really loved during chemo, because it may be the last time I'd love them. There were literal prayers that eggs and avocados would taste the same. Thankfully, I was able to manage those two things once I was at least seven days post-infusion. Mostly, my diet consisted of instant mashed potatoes, a pancake, or a banana mashed up with peanut butter and a drizzle of pancake syrup. Got that little recipe from a mouth cancer patient. It gets rid of the metal mouth taste that many experience. Some things made me incredibly sick and still do, to this day. Unless I make the red pasta or pizza sauce fresh myself, it makes me sick.

Anyway, sweet tea changed the game on day four. It provided a brief period of partial alertness in which I could accomplish a couple of things. Showering would HAVE to be one of those this time. I had about three weeks, and radiation would begin.

More learning was on the way!

## *May 3: Radiation simulation and start*

**Natalie McCoy**
May 3, 2024 · 🔒

Chemo Complete . On to the next step here at home. Radiation time! Thank you, isn't enough to explain how grateful I am for all of you. The messages, cards, gifts, visits, etc. Have really kept my joy alive. I'm not done with this journey & I don't know that any survivor is really done but radiation brings me closer. Ready to get it done!

❤️👍😮 98                                                     15 comments

Radiation is every day, Monday through Friday, for about an hour a day, so I opted to do this treatment at home to avoid having to move to Florida for the six weeks of treatment. Radiation simulation is an interesting appointment where they measure and mark you to prepare for your first round. I was scheduled for twenty-five rounds, and when I say "measure and mark," that meant I got three small blue dot tattoos. Yes, they're permanent, but they're tiny, and I already have tattoos, so it was fine with me. You talk through how you'll be positioned on the table. My particular treatment would require me to hold my breath for about thirty seconds at a time for several rounds while the radiation was administered. I had practiced breath holds in physical therapy in preparation for this because I was so tired from chemo that I struggled to hold my breath for more than nine seconds.

## *July 2: Radiation Bell Ringing. That's right! Another Bell!*

**Natalie McCoy**
July 2, 2024 · 🔒

Hey Friends! Its bell ringing graduation day #2! My video wouldn't load but today I completed the acute phase of treatment & I rang the bell for radiation! I still have treatment to do & many appointments ahead but almost a year after my diagnosis I can say I've completed the 3 big steps: surgery, chemo & radiation are behind me. It's been the hardest 10 months of my life but my spirit prevailed because God is good. I have the best family, friends, church group & doctors a person could want & I'm thankful for all of you & all the support!

Tomorrow I see oncology & we'll see what the next steps are!

❤ 👍 ✌ 275     65 comments

New side effects come with radiation, including radiation burn that would set in on my chest and neck a few days after that post. While it sucked, I felt like it was nothing compared to chemo, and I was just happy to be here. I was traveling to Florida to see my oncologist the next day, and I was ready to hear the words "Cancer Free". I had become close to my oncologist, as I'm sure many patients do, but she had become a friend as well as my teammate. Back in round three of chemo, Rose made me a shirt that said "My oncologist does my hair," and I started wearing it on infusion days. The first time I wore it, my oncologist walked into my treatment room already giggling because the nurses told her what it said. I told her I would get her a shirt that said, "Doing hair is my side hustle." She is a sweet soul who has found her calling in life and is living it out with purpose. I can't say enough good things about her, and I was excited to see her the next day!

## *July 3: SURVIVOR DAY*

**Natalie McCoy**
July 3, 2024 · 👤

···

Today is special y'all. I move into maintenance phase for treatment & today I can say I'm a SURVIVOR!!!! "Cancer free" is a powerful phrase I've been waiting to hear & today it rang in my ears! MD Anderson is a special place & I'm forever thankful to God that he placed us here with MD.

1 more plug for y'all: V for Victory is a non-profit organization that supports those battling Cancer in the area. They've provided a LOT for me & my family over the past 10 months. If you find it in your heart; look them up & learn about them!

❤️👍🥰 223

49 comments

She told me the words I went to hear.

"Congratulations, you're cancer-free."

She hugged me and told me she was proud of me and proud to know me. Proud to know me?? I thought. Ma'am, I'm proud to know you. You're the life-saver of this friendship! She laid out my next steps. I would begin my medication regimen as soon as the prescriptions were filled. That was the long-term plan. I would give myself an injection every twenty-eight days,

I would take one pill for ten years (medical menopause), and I would take another chemo pill for two years that showed promising results in aiding in the reduction of the chance of recurrence. There's a ton more to this appointment, but that's the quick and dirty version. More appointments, more surgeries, and starting the process of being in medical menopause were to come. It's AWFUL if you're wondering. I don't think anyone expects it to be a good time. I just never thought I'd be doing it at age forty. Ladies—do your research on perimenopause and menopause. You're not crazy; weird things do happen, so make sure you're paying attention and take care of yourself.

But y'all—It was *survivor* day, and that's all that mattered.

My husband was in a meeting at work when I left the appointment, and I knew he would be out soon. I went across the street to a pizza place to eat before I made the drive home. I sat there, alone, wanting to jump for joy and cry all at the same time. It was like time was in slow motion for me, but fast forward for everyone in the pizza place around me. I took my phone out and texted Josey. It said, "Guess what frand! I'm cancer-free & today I became a survivor!" I sent her the picture with the hope rock.

I teared up as I typed it and tried to hide the tears because I was in a pizza place after all. It wasn't lost on me that I'd told Josey before my own husband, but she's a sister. My kindred soul friend knew everything about me. She'd called me after infusions and just sat on the phone with me in silence, sometimes just so I wouldn't be alone. She texted me the cutest ways to wear head coverings and earrings, she sent me infusion shirts to wear during chemo, magnetic eyelashes because she knows I'm allergic to adhesives, a wig, stamp-on eyebrows, and so much more. She just understood me enough to know what I needed, when I needed it, and without ever talking to me about it. So, I texted her first. She didn't text back right away (she works from home), and I thought, well, she's on a call or something. A couple of minutes went by, and she called me. I answered, "heeey." And there was almost complete silence. I looked at the screen to make sure it hadn't hung up, and as I put the phone back to my ear, she squeaked out the words through obvious, big tears, "I'm so proud of you. You did it." Now I sat in a pizza place crying. We both got through the first few sentences and then giggled and talked for a bit. It was surreal. She knew this wasn't the end of treatment. But she was right, I had finished the hardest part. She stuck with me when things were ugly. She was one of the few that I told all the terrible side effects to; she let me vent when people made me mad, and she knew the real deal. The reality of what treatment looks like. I have years and years of treatment ahead and decades to wonder if it'll come back. That's in the back of every survivor's mind all the time. But Josey had really gone through it with me. And when she could tell I didn't want to talk about it anymore, she would change the subject and we'd move on.

I have a few friends who stuck with me through this whole journey, and I'd be remiss if I didn't mention them too. Club Langley ladies were all there, my best friend from high school made shirts and sent them to my family, my best friend from college made a trip to Georgia to see me during treatment, and my best friend from graduate school did the same! The ladies in my Connect group came and held my family together through the rough stuff, and the friends I made who are local have become very close to me. These ladies are amazing, and every woman needs to find themselves some like em.

Again, the ones who show up when things are hard, not when it's convenient for them. They'll take your kids for you, come over in sweatpants with no make-up, and their hair half done in an instant.

*July 26: Port Removal Procedure*

 **Natalie McCoy**
July 26, 2024 · 🎗

Cancer is to be defeated by the Relentless! In an hour, my Port comes OUT! For some reason this procedure has me a little shook up. But it's because this Port has carried life-saving medicine/poison through me for months now and today I say goodbye to it.....hopefully this is a 1-time partnership with me & this Port. I appreciated it but I hope & pray I never encounter it again!!!!

Head up, eyes open & move forward friends!

❤️👍💬 230                                    43 comments

This day was a struggle! I was supposed to be more excited than anything, but what I would later know is that what I was experiencing was grief. My port was coming out, and that was one more step towards normal life again, but I was sad. I was scared. What if the cancer came back and I didn't have my port to immediately get treatment? It didn't make sense to me that I felt that way.

The only way to describe it was to compare it to a specific scene from one of my favorite movies because it's the picture I had in my head. If you've seen *Apollo 13*, you may understand. It's the scene where the astronauts have moved out of the LEM and back into their command module as they're preparing to return home. It shows the three of them looking through a small window at the LEM as they cut it loose into space to float around forever and never be seen again. They discuss how she saved them and how she was a good ship as she floats away. That's how this port coming out felt. The thing that had saved me and become part of my body had to go.

During the removal procedure, I was only partially sedated, so they x-rayed my chest before and asked me what I saw. I said, "I see a port on the right side of my chest." Then they performed the removal, completed another X-ray, and showed it to me again, asking what I saw. I almost couldn't get the words out, and I got choked up, but didn't want them to know. I replied, "It's gone."

I told my husband how I felt, and he said he understood but that he wanted me to be excited. Later that evening, I would make a shocking (to me) discovery. I was showering and I noticed that I didn't see one of my tattoos. No, I'm not going to tell you where it was located, but it was literally gone. I freaked out. I immediately got out and went to my husband and said, "Hey, my tattoo is gone. Did you know it was gone?" He stared at me like I was CRAZY and said, "Yes (kind of giggling), it's been gone since your first surgery eight months ago. Did you seriously just notice it was gone?" Yep, that's right. I had blocked out so much in the process of putting my head down and grinding that I hadn't even noticed that a whole tattoo was gone. He told me that he thought I should really consider talking to a therapist because he had assumed I had known it was gone.

Without going into depth, I did seek out a trauma therapist, and it was worth every minute. It propelled me forward.

## *September 12: Reflection on One Year Post-Diagnosis*

 **Natalie McCoy**
September 12, 2024 · 👥

Go back with me 1 YEAR!  It's 1am on 9/12/23, Steve & I sit in an ER, 24 hours into a PCS thinking I have a lung infection. Instead, we hear, "there's no good way to go over this so here we go. We're confident that you have Breast Cancer."

We didn't talk or cry. I had 8,786 questions but didn't know what any of them were. My heart shattered when we told our kids.

ONE WHOLE YEAR has passed. I have a husband who is a solid rock. There aren't enough words to thank him. He is pure Gold.

Y'ALL, I'm HERE!  The enemy DID NOT steal my joy, my drive or my life. God is good all the time and all the time God is good. This was always his plan for me and now he's guiding me through part 2 of this journey; encouraging & supporting those that are at the beginning and still in the nightmare phase.

Isaiah 41:10 : "Fear Not. For I am with you. Do not be afraid, for I am your God. I will strengthen you and hold you up with my righteous right hand."

It seems odd to celebrate a diagnosis day, but I had made it 1 year from the day that altered who I was, the body I lived in, and the life I had, so I posted about it. The year of FIRSTS was in progress!

❤️👍😢 192                                                           49 comments

## *January 11: One Year Since First Chemo Reflection Post*

 **Natalie McCoy**
January 11, 2025 · 👥

There I sit, 1 mo. post-op in a new body I didn't recognize, jaw clenched. Perseverance was/is my repeated word of choice but I learned that perseverance is messy. It's waking up some days, head down & grinding & then it's stumbling, sometimes falling but it must always be rising after the fall. Because if you don't rise, you give up and giving up will not be associated with me. Perseverance is the constant pursuit of improvement. But it's reaching the summit of a difficult mountain thinking you'll be relieved, only to find it's the first peak in a mountain range. Perseverance is self-awareness, discipline, reflection and knowing that truly living begins when stop the noise & pray. Really, truly, genuinely pray. For everything and anything. Today- I'm at the mountain top overlooking the mountain range that is cancer. Cancer is a constant climb, a marathon & a life endeavor. It's not over when you ring a bell...it's only just beginning. But I know that my mountain range has many peaks remaining & my creator has a plan for me so I'll keep climbing & praying. I'm here for anyone that wants to talk or ask questions! Go & live & do it as your best self!

❤️👍😢 110                                                           31 comments

*February 14: My Birthday*

**Natalie McCoy**
February 14, 2025 ·

I thought turning 40 would be awful, but I'm just happy to be here at 40!! Yesterday was the best 40th birthday I could have asked for! Thank you to everyone who texted & messaged me. After a year of surgery, chemo, radiation & physical therapy I was able to do my 1st deadlifts yesterday since 2023!!!! Lots of you made my birthday awesome, drank coffee, did nails, went to lunch & dinner with me & showed up with my favorite things as gifts! 40 AIN'T SO BAD PEOPLE! It's the start of a new era & I plan to whoop this decade into submission! VALENTINE'S MAFIA FOR LIFE!

 140                                    66 comments

There was a time when I wondered if I would see forty and if I did see forty would I be sick and fighting, would I have hair? What would forty look like?

*April 4: Month of the Military Child Post*

**Natalie McCoy**
April 4, 2025 ·

It's April! Month of the Military child is upon us!

These amazing kids of ours have accomplished so much in their short lives. Military kids are special, they are resilience beyond their years, they're patient, they're cultured & well rounded, they're mature, they have deeper understanding of the world than most and they are living history out as a part of the world's greatest military. They go through things most kids will never face, they move every few years & learn how to start completely over. They have friends ALL over the world. Ingrained in them is how to make friends into family and then never leave that family behind.

I'll say it again- THEY ARE RESILIENT!

I am SO proud of my girls. They've overcome a PCS that went directly into overcoming cancer with me, we're almost through our first year of middle school, they've started sports, sewing classes, youth group praise team at church & saying see you later to friends we love.

The color of the month is PURPLE (the color of all military branches combined) & the symbol, a DANDELION. Cause these kids bloom wherever they land!

Purple Up peeps!

 108                                    17 comments

You'll see many posts like this in April from military parents everywhere. We're all proud of our kids and who they are, and we all like to celebrate them appropriately because they didn't choose to be in a family that serves, but they embrace it!

*June 24: Phase Two - Reconstruction*

**Natalie McCoy**
June 24, 2025 ·

"I don't have a soul, I am a soul. I have a body." (Unknown)

I am a soul & spirit full of happiness, love, fierce loyalty, trust & most of all: HOPE. I pray that what memories I leave my kids are those of feisty hope. Memories of their mom's dedication to following truth & loving others well. This body that I have has been through more than I could have ever imagined by age 40. We've fought through a lot together & Today- I'm a step closer to normal again (new normal anyway). It's reconstruction day!!!!!! Today is finally a happy day in the journey of Cancer. See y'all on the flip side in my upgraded body that carries who I really am in spirit.

❤️ 👍 🏆 262                                                   67 comments

I finally reached reconstruction surgery day, phase two. The wait had been so long, and I was so excited to get it over with. My body and my life were on track to return to some normalcy once this piece was complete.

Life would never look the same again, and I was ready to move on from being a patient all the time. I didn't want to be known for cancer. I have lots of physical restrictions from my arms and chest, not being able to move properly anymore. I have joint pain every day from the chemo pills, sometimes severe.

Through it all, I am alive. My kids have their mama, my husband still has a wife, and I am thankful. My mind was becoming slightly clearer, even though brain fog still exists, and I started contemplating what was next.

*July 3: First Cancerversary*

**Natalie McCoy**
July 3, 2025 ·

I thought today was going to be chill but these people showed up SO BIG to celebrate with me. They surprised me in the best way!!! Love y'all.

💗👍💬 225                                                          29 comments

This day I had waited for, thought about, and reflected on. My best friend from college was on her second trip visiting me. Neither of us knew that my local Georgia friends had set up a huge surprise dinner for me. My husband texted me to say that he'd taken care of dinner and he'd come pick us up later.

This dinner was magical for me. I had made it a whole year from the words *cancer free* and got to celebrate with a bunch of balloons, cupcakes, a GIANT table of tacos (my favorite) and big group of friends. Yet even in the joy of that day, a quiet question lingered in my mind:

How do I move forward, and what does that look like?

God had walked with me through the valley and brought me out the other side, but what do I do with it? I began to really pray and repeatedly ask,

"What do you want me to do with this journey?"

I can't have survived purely because I'm stubborn; there must be a reason.

# 9

## IF YOU MUST BE BALD, BE BOLD: THE UNKNOWN PROMOTES FEAR

The reason I'm here is that I was made for more, made to do more, made to pray more, made to help others more, made to act, not just talk. If you've never listened to the song "*Made for More*," Run, don't walk, and turn it on. It has become my theme song, and it speaks truth into my life as a reminder that I wasn't made to sit, tend my grave, and wait for death.

To revisit the thoughts I shared about losing my hair, I will say that there was a turning point for me. Once the hair was out, that was it. There was no turning back. I was bald. I didn't like it, but I couldn't change it, so I decided to be bold about it. I took Josey's advice and the thirty packs of earrings she sent, and I started finding scarves I liked to wear. I learned several ways to wear them, and I adopted big earrings, hoop earrings, and sparkly earrings. Earrings that made people look at me. I'd rather someone look right at me than try to avoid eye contact, so they don't appear to be staring and wondering. I could not live in fear of what others would think or say. I had to own it; all of it. Living in the unknown perpetuates an attitude of anxiety, maybe sadness, and depression, and it crushes opportunities for growth. Facing the unknown, regardless of what that represents for you, must eventually happen. I choose to get it over with as soon as I notice it.

The unknown could be many things. It could be wondering what people will think of you when you have no hair or constantly trying to shut out thoughts about the cancer coming back. That will be a lifelong debate in my head that I'll be trying to quiet. The unknown could be walking across the street to introduce yourself to a new neighbor, so they feel welcome even though you're an introvert and don't want to talk to anyone. All introverts need an extrovert and vice versa—go find each other. You'll be happy you did.

For Josey and me, it's become one of the strongest friendships we have, and it won't fade. If you're a military spouse. FOR sure, face the unknown of meeting your neighbors. You too could find a Club Langley. I know those neighborhoods exist overseas and there are some stateside, but they are few and far between. Go and create them! Maybe you're unknown is deciding to finally talk to someone at the gym, even though they look like a meat-head or a gym rat—whichever phrase you prefer. Many times, people are amazing, but we all tend to look angry when we're in the zone working out. Disregard people's faces when they're working out, and go talk to them. A piece of gym etiquette, though: do not stop them in the middle of a set to talk, you might lose a friend instead of gaining one.

My personal favorite fear to face now that my brain has basically been wiped and I can't remember much, is asking people their names after I've been talking to them for months on end. At work, in the neighborhood, at church; it doesn't matter. That one never gets less awkward, but Y'ALL! You need to know folks' names; you're going to have to ask. They might be in the same boat and just not want to ask you either. It'll be a bonding experience for the both of you.

Lots of people just follow routine. I've learned as a military spouse that locals don't realize they aren't talking to you. It makes you feel like you're the outsider, because you are. But they don't realize that, and they most often don't mean for you to feel that way. I said before that I have been told that someone wouldn't be friends with me because we're military, and we'll just leave, so they don't waste their time.

OK, fine, your loss, Ruby Sue. I don't know a Ruby Sue—I just like to throw names in places when I talk. For example, if I don't know your middle name and I feel the need to use it. It'll be Marie every time. I don't care if you're a dude.

My point is this:

Locals are doing their thing like they have their entire lives. They aren't trying to exclude you; they're just used to doing everything with family and their friends they've had since Pre-K. They've had these friend groups forever, and here we come as military spouses looking for friends and hoping maybe they'll adopt us, but that's hard for them, and weird. And to us, we're offended. Like, I know I'm likable. I'm a good time. What's wrong with them? Well, you are likable and you're a great time, but they don't know that and it's risky for them to bring you into an established friend group. Now I get that, but it's taken me 15+ years.

My first time having local friends was when cancer forced me upon them, and they adopted me. So, it's two-fold. My advice to military spouses, especially young and early in your military career is to find other military spouses and be there for each other. Don't omit the opportunity for local friends, but lean hard into your military family. They're experiencing life in the same way you are, and locals have no comparison for that. How could they? Trust me when I tell you that your military spouse friends are lifelong. You'll find yourself traveling to see one another once you all PCS. The upside there is that it provides opportunities to travel to new places. Silver lining, right?!

Now that I'm a seasoned (I'm twenty-nine in my head, so I won't say old) military spouse and I have fought the fight of my life, I've leaned into local friends, and it was a learning process for me. These chicks are cool. I liked them and they took me in; I'm sure cautiously at first, but they played it off well. I'm at a point in my life where these girls are really living life with me. We go to church together, events together, dinner (and sometimes only dessert) together, and we go on trips together. I was able to teach them just like they taught me. I'm used to being up for a girl's trip on a whim or stopping everything to travel to a friend in need. That's somewhat new to them. Everyone who's important in their lives lives close, and they see each other regularly. The thought of going on a girls' trip blew some of their minds because their husbands weren't used to it. Not that the husbands were opposed to it—it was just a new idea. I'll say it again; I thrive in uncomfortable situations, and I like to apply positive peer pressure when I know good will come from it. So, I've gotten these locals out of their comfort zones, and they have done the same for me.

As I grew closer to my newfound local friends, I had an encounter with one of them that shook me. She made me consider the local girl's emotions and logic in a new light, even though I thought I understood. I left her house one evening, we hugged, and she said, "love ya, see ya later!" Upon arriving home, I checked my phone and saw a text from her that said, "So, will the military take you away from me one day??" In all the years, I had never really understood the emotions associated with the other side. I didn't like hearing that people didn't want to be friends with me because we're military, but it's a protective factor for them. It's painful. It broke my heart when I read that text. It also overwhelmed me with joy and gratitude for her. She actually liked me, loved me even—enough to be worried that I would leave. You have to decide for yourself what your friend group will consist of, but cast your net wide in your search and be picky about who your keepers are. You want good influences that pour into you equally what you pour into them.

Just don't let the fear of the unknown consume you!

# 10

## THE PEOPLE FROM THE WOODWORKS

*"There is no one so good they don't need God's
grace and no one so bad they can't have it"*

- Paraphrased from Tim Keller

We were building our new community of friends in Georgia, and it seemed like it was easier than ever before. We really found our place in our church, and we grew as a family. The way we follow Christ now makes the rest of our lives almost a joke. We just weren't living it before. We believed in it, and we had salvation, but we weren't executing the mission correctly. We weren't living it, and now it was time to do so. What did I have to lose? I had been to the edge of death and back. God allowed me to sit in that place, and in that, I found myself again, who I really am, and I can clearly see what I'm supposed to be doing. I can't turn it off now. I can't and I won't stop this train of happiness and the overflow of love I feel.

All these people at church had just come from nowhere—like out of the woodworks, to show up and clean my house during chemo, feed us, pray for us, and had gotten us involved in things at church. When the hard treatments ended, they didn't disappear back into the woods; they kept showing up. Pretty cool. I would still have a hard time on Sunday mornings because I just couldn't get all the words to the songs out without choking up. It bothered me, made me mad even. I was feeling more like myself, and myself doesn't like tears but does like singing loudly, usually when nobody else has to hear it.

On a Sunday following the service, a lady stopped me and said, "When are you going to go to choir?" Choir? I thought. Is she for real? This is a joke.

Turns out I said that out loud. Thought it was in my head, but nope. She heard me, and now we were looking at each other.

She said, "Can you make a joyful noise?"

"I can't sing," I replied.

She said, "I didn't ask if you could sing. Can you make a noise and do you have joy in the Lord?"

"Uhhhhh, yeah, I guess. And yes, I have joy in the Lord." I said.

Come on, ma'am. She was challenging me. It felt slightly competitive, maybe confrontational in nature, even though I knew she didn't mean it like that.

"Well, then. You can join the choir. You'll be fine. Come on. Just come give it a try once."

I never considered being in the choir before. I mulled it over for a couple of weeks and mentioned it to the therapist I was still seeing. The therapist thought it was a great idea. She thought it would help me to sing my chemo song. The song I struggled with the most. Even if I cried, she wanted me to get it out. Honestly, I didn't expect her to agree that joining the choir would be a good thing. Sunday rolls around, and a third person mentions choir to me.

What is it with these people and the choir?

I mean, don't get me wrong. I loved the music and worship at church. It was always perfect in terms of timing and presence, and the Worship Pastor was fantastic. He was on fire about what his mission was in life, and it was noticeable.

I considered attending a choir practice for weeks. I thought, "They don't know me well. They don't know how terrible my mouth was just two years prior." I learned to block out the noise and the need to cuss over the course of the PCS and treatment. I had prayed about needing intervention for my mouth for probably five years, but I hadn't started truly living for the Lord until our PCS. It was amazing how my mouth naturally calmed when I surrendered to what God's plan was for me, and it became harder TO cuss than not to. But nobody around me knew that I was a terrible Christian before. Why would they be OK with me singing?

And it hit me. Not one person in that choir loft is without fault or sin. None of them. They were all up there as broken people just doing what the Bible tells us to do, worship.

Ok, ok, ok. I could at least go to one practice and see how I felt about it. It was SO MUCH FUN. Here I was thinking about choir and music as if it required choir robes, perfect pitches, and solely old hymns. I'm not even sure why I thought that. I was there on Sundays, and I knew what they sang. My brain just hadn't considered the possibility of ever doing it, so there was no prior thought. Old hymns are still sung in our church, but there's a mix of old and new in a way that flows for generations; old and new. It's cohesive, affording the opportunity for all to worship.

There was no turning back; I was hooked. Only three weeks would pass before my chemo song appeared in the planned music for the week. Nervousness to sing it from the choir loft was ever-present. The morning of, I told a friend my dilemma about being afraid to cry, and she said, "Who cares. We all cry up there sometimes. Get up here and sing it like you mean it."

It was freeing. I could feel anxiety melting away because I knew I was singing it from where I was supposed to be. It was a beautiful experience, and my friend (a local chick) who told me to get up there side-hugged me while we sang it together.

People had shown up in my life when I needed them most. Some to challenge me in doing things (like choir), some to support me in times of greatest need (like my Connect group), and some to live life with me in an intimate way (like Club Langley and my newfound local chicks).

Each occurrence molded my thoughts differently from the previous. I don't trust easily and never have. Early on in life, I was gullible, and that was the last time I trusted people right out of the gate. I don't search for the negative in others by any means, but I look far and wide for people to talk to, and I like to include everybody. People have to give me a reason to question them now instead of me instantly assuming they all have ulterior motives. This process had softened me a bit.

I've become so accustomed to being in choir now that the weeks feel longer when I miss a Sunday or even a Wednesday practice. Worshipping with song is my favorite way to worship. My choir people are my PEOPLE. You want to jam out with people ready to sing and dance at the drop of a hat? Church choir is the place! We joke about keeping toe tams on us in case a praise break pops off in the parking lot. It's just a good time, all the time, because God is good.

Throughout my existence, people entered the picture at the right moment with the right momentum for the situations I was in, and they've carried me through all in their own ways. That kind of stuff happens for a reason. It happens because I'm a believer who allows myself to be guided by my intuition. I follow through when I feel nudged by that "inner gut feeling" telling me to do, or not do, something. Because the Holy Spirit does not fail in guidance.

I spent my early years rooted in being a Christian, and I can't say that I chose to walk away from that life because that's not it. I simply allowed the world to become too influential in my life. I partied too much, I cussed too much, I made bad choices (surprise—all Christians do), I wronged people at times, and I was wronged. Ultimately, in the firestorm that consumed me, called cancer, I found my way home. Back to Christ, because I'm forgiven simply because he loves me and died for me. It's that simple.

I absolutely know there are people out there who don't like me to this day, and while I hope they've forgiven me if I wronged them, I also know that I'm not for everybody. I'm a distinct personality with no chill; I'm always on, and I can overwhelm those who are introverted. I'm loud, I'm stern, and I'm direct. Once I decide that I'm going to do something, it's happening. I say what I mean and I mean what I say. I will follow through, and I hope people know that I will do everything in my power to show up when they're in need, regardless of whether we're friends or not.

As a part of the list of things I teach my kids is: Not everyone will like you, and that's OK. You won't like everyone. But what isn't an option is how you treat those people, even the ones who don't like you. We teach our kids (and remind ourselves) that we are not on this earth to judge, gossip, or single out any one person or group of people. We are on this earth to love thy neighbor as thyself. PERIOD. Not just when it's convenient, but when it's the hardest. God takes care of the rest. Our mission is one of actionable love. You will never look into the eyes of a person that God didn't create. Remember that.

The random people coming in and out of my life had come in and out for reasons. Some stayed. Some were only for a moment in time, but they all poured into me and taught me life lessons I needed to learn. Those lessons have fine-tuned me into who I am today. Some lessons were hard, some I didn't want to learn, but all were necessary. I've had bosses who only taught me how NOT to supervise people. There's a lesson in that, too.

And you know what? Learning that early in my career made me a supervisor who cares and listens to employees. I enjoy taking care of people, especially when they are part of my team. By the grace of God, I have honed the spiritual gift of leading people, and prayerfully, I'll continue to do so.

One of the things EVERY person holds within them is potential. If you're a Christian, that potential should be viewed and can transform into what we call spiritual gifts. Figuring out what those gifts are can change your life in an enormously fulfilling way. Turning that gift into a craft and shaping it into daily life, your job, and serving your community can change the lives of others. That grace and love will multiply.

The last team I worked with referred to me by several names other than my legal one. Over time, looking back on those, I saw that they had helped me identify my spiritual gifts. They called me "The Glue," "The Sheriff," and "The Cat Herder," most often. But in each of those lies a personality trait I see value in. I like bringing people together and connecting people who need to know each other. I enjoy showing hospitality in a way that binds people together, hence—The Glue. If you or we as a team need something accomplished and there are roadblocks, I'm ya girl. I could walk into a meeting, present my facts and reasoning for why we needed whatever it was, and almost 100% of the time, I got it. Even if someone had been asking for it for five years and had been told no. I don't like being told no without reason. If you have a good reason, but the justification is old, I'll also research how to correct that, hence—The Sheriff. My team was spread out all over the base, working on multiple things all at once. We thrived under pressure, and we prided ourselves on producing results, not sometimes, but every time. I was always prepared with information about where each team member was on any given day, what results they were working towards, and why we had chosen to be where we were. I never knew who was going to question me, so I just stayed ready—hence The Cat Herder.

Stop and think about that.

Real talk: What are you good at and how can it help others? There is peace and joy in using your gifts to help others. Yes, even when you don't like people in general.

Since we're here, let's try this little exercise. Grab a piece of paper and write down three things you believe you are good at. Not things that others have told you you're good at, although those may concur with your own thoughts. These things should be something you believe you truly excel at or could excel at, provided the opportunity, whether you've ever told anyone about them or not. Write them down and keep them. These are skills and personality traits. They may be practical. They may also be intangible.

Some examples might be:

Teaching

Hospitality

Singing

Caring for children

Wealth

Business ownership

Playing Instruments

Making others feel secure

Cooking and Baking—people love cookies, let's be honest

Praying for others

Helping the elderly

Helping the Homeless and less fortunate

Helping Foster Kids find their way

This is the short list to give you an idea of how broad and wide you should think, but know this. You have skills, whether you identify them as such or not. You will never be able to use them if you can't identify them.

People came from the woodworks and used their skills to impact me throughout my life in ways I cannot disregard. Cancer redirected my energy and efforts, reminded me that I once rose from the baptism waters as a new person, and that girl must continue living. I'm not living for myself now. My days are numbered, as all our days are, but I feel a sense of urgency with my days that I didn't feel before cancer. I always assumed I'd have time to get back into church and find my way using my gifts. Cancer is eye-opening, and it plants the seed that the time is NOW. It's time to love people big, show up when people need me, pray for people (most are ok with that), and be with my kids. It's time to love and serve my own family well, my military family well, and my biblical community well.

The people from the woodworks walked up to my front door with meals, gift cards, and prayers. They may never know how much they impacted me. Well, hopefully they'll read this, and now they know! They inspired me. They are part of the spark that lit the flame in me. They continue to add fuel so that the fire rages internally.

One of my favorite quotes is:

*"To give less than the best is to sacrifice a gift."* -Steve Prefontaine

I've always found that to be profound. I was in high school when I first heard it. I was a cross-country runner and heard this because of who Steve Prefontaine was. It stuck with me because it was the first time I questioned myself about giving my all in everything I did. Why would we give less than our best to anything? If you're going to do something, do it all the way and to your best ability.

My grandfather was extremely influential in my life in the best way possible. He always told me that if I had the ability to do something, I had the responsibility to do it. Especially if it pertained to impacting another living being. That is deeply ingrained in my moral code, and I live by it.

As a survivor, I have the responsibility to support others in the same cancer battle that I have overcome. I have the responsibility to educate and support younger military spouses because this life is hard, and I refuse to accept the premise that "I had to learn it the hard way. So should they."

No. Nope. Uhh Uhh. That's wrong all day long and twice on Tuesday.

I learned it the hard way, and now it's my turn to take that knowledge and help somebody else. The phrase "because we've always done it that way" is deadly. It sucks the life from the room, and it stops progress in its tracks. People poured into my life, and that shaped my integrity. Their words and actions helped create the internal drive I have to search for people in need.

I've talked about my cancer buddies. My cancer buddies are warriors, some of them quite literally. They are active-duty members, some are military spouses, some are children, and some are caregivers of those warriors. We stand shoulder to shoulder with each other, ready to catch anyone who falls.

Make no mistake—my cancer buddies and I are at war with our own bodies. Some of us will win, some of us will win temporarily, and some of us will succumb. We are at war with our thoughts, our beliefs, our truth, our path, and our guilt. I have survivor's guilt that sometimes overcomes me. I've had four panic attacks, or what I think were panic attacks. The first was during chemo, but the other three? Those were the first and second times I directly faced family members of someone who had just passed away from cancer. The third was listening to someone speak about the one-year anniversary of their brother's death from cancer. All I could think was they must be looking at me and wondering why I was here, and their loved one was gone. I felt like the whole room was staring at me. I know that's not at all how people really felt. I wasn't being realistic, but an overwhelming sense of guilt hits me, and probably will for years to come, in that situation.

As I write this, I think of my many cancer buddies and how we each came to know each other. It was no accident, and every instance is noteworthy in its own story. The good Lord knows we need each other. Nobody can understand a cancer patient except a cancer patient. Nobody. Not their parents, not their caregiver or spouse. Only another cancer patient.

I continue meeting people who are entering the fight and survivors of the fight. Oftentimes, I happen across them in random circumstances. When I'm presented the opportunity, especially if it's a random interaction, that's my sign—draw them in and love on them.

It has become my lifelong side-hustle. No matter where I work, I will forever be gathering more cancer buddies, and we will fight together, hopefully to victory.

# 11

## THE REALITY OF SURVIVORSHIP WITH PRACTICAL APPLICATION

Surviving cancer is an achievement, but what happens after that?

You don't just move on like nothing happened. Years of appointments, medications, and wondering what's wrong every time a bone hurts or you get a cough you can't explain lie ahead. Once you're cancer-free, it means finding a way to navigate mental health that is productive, not just shoving down all the feelings to make them go away.

So, what now? You survived. Most people assumed you were fine as soon as the initial treatment was over, and they all moved on, even though your world stood still. Now you live in a world you may not know how to navigate. I know I didn't.

My body is no longer physically capable of doing things that my mind says it can still do, and sometimes I'm not aware of that until I'm trying to load my truck bed full of garden soil, and I either get exhausted quickly, I can't lift anymore, or I have a hot flash. I forget that my entire chest wall was opened up, my body was destroyed with chemotherapy, and I still take medications that cause severe fatigue, lung problems, swelling in my limbs, the potential for lymphedema, and so on.

This is when learning who you are now versus who you are in your mind is incredibly difficult. It's depressing when you find things you can no longer do the same because the range of motion in your joints is gone after radiation therapy. I get angry every time I drop things because I have permanent neuropathy in my fingertips from chemo, and I'm sporadically nauseous; usually at terrible times like when I'm driving or having a conversation.

I must remind myself that there was a point in this journey when I was unable to use an apple slicer and today, I can. It took time. At least five times, I arrived at a point where I truly believed that the progress I had made was all I would make. Then I went further.

It's having a new mindset: just because I can do something doesn't mean I should.

The constant education leveled me up in survivorship. The practical application phase, where new living begins!

You should know by now that I like a list. A tangible thing I can use to gauge progress, boost memory, or provide reminders. Below, I'm going to share some updates to lifestyle my family has implemented. Some dietary things we've changed, and the conversations we've had about how to improve our overall health. This isn't just about me. This is for all of us.

My husband and I have always cooked at home most, if not every, night of the week. We use healthy ingredients and pay attention to how we shop, but there's always room for improvement. Broadening the scope of recipes and learning how nutrition impacts our quality of life leads me to share the simple changes we made. So super easy that anyone can do it. I'm not a dietitian, so you won't find recipes here. That's not really my point anyway.

My background in healthcare, health and wellness, and sports medicine has afforded me educational opportunities that are relevant. At a minimum, I stay engaged in health and wellness so I know what's available. My survivorship team integrates holistic and alternative medicine into my survival treatment plan. Most of these things do not deal with diet, and some are mental health-related, but they're all easy. These are my family's choices. You can do some of them, or none. My point is: do your own research, and get it from verified sources. Just because it's on social media doesn't make it true.

Our family approach:

- Swapped out all plastic plates, cups, and bowls for glass.

- Swapped all food storage containers from plastic to glass.

- Do our best (sometimes price dictates) to only buy things that are sold in glass containers at the grocery store.

- Swapped all cutting boards to glass.

- Swapped out cookware from non-stick to stainless steel, cast iron, or ceramic. *There are others, but do your research and find what you like.

- Swapped cooking utensils for wooden ones.

- Minimize or avoid fast-food places altogether. For a variety of reasons, but down to the packaging the food comes in, it's not good for you.

- Researched and purchased different dish soap, laundry soap, and hygiene products.

- Swapped lawn products out after researching chemicals.

- When using things like eye drops buy the ones without preservatives if you can.

- My favorite of the whole list! Grow your own food! Plant a garden! I have a decent garden. I plant seeds in the winter and start them inside, then move them when they're ready to be outside. I get them into good soil and water away. Plant a variety of foods that your family eats the most, and you can get a good-sized harvest. You'll get to eat stuff as you pick it. You can pickle it, can it, freeze it, dehydrate it, etc. Find your growing zone, learn how to plant in it, and give it a try. It's easy and incredibly rewarding. I don't use chemicals in my garden, and I have it set up to self-water. We eat from it regularly. My kids have learned about healthy eating simply from planting and harvesting.

The garden is for mental and physical health. It feels good to watch my kids try new recipes and learn to cook things that we grow. Kids are more likely to try new foods if they pick them, too. It allows space outside, in the sun, soaking up some Vitamin D with fresh air. It's good for your brain, your skin, and your body. It provides a space where you can be active with your hands while your mind wanders off to calmly deal with its thoughts. Listen to music while you work and let the garden teach you.

- Growing your own is the best, but if you aren't ready for that or don't have enough space yet, pay attention to where your food comes from, research chemicals used on crops, and decide if that changes how you purchase produce. Container gardens can be very successful if you have limited space.

- Learn your area, your local farmers and ranchers, and know what they have to offer. If you can find a butcher or rancher that sells meat, figure out how you can buy a quarter or half of an animal instead of buying meat in the grocery store. The quality is better, many times its more cost effective and you know where your meat came from.

- Buy blocks of cheese and we shred it ourselves. It's cheaper and has a lot less ingredients.

- When making coffee, we either make a pour-over or we put loose coffee grounds into a stainless-steel reusable cup container that goes into the single-serve cup machine. Get rid of the plastic reusable and the single-use cups if you can. Cheaper and better.

- Implement more Mediterranean dishes. We try to do one day a week with no meat.

- Use only lean meats, and add more fish. Here's a weird chemo thing for you—I hated fish most of my life. After chemo, I started to crave fish, so now we eat it more. It's good for everyone!

- An easy way to ensure you're getting less processed food is to just shop around the edges of the grocery store. That's usually where all the fresh items are. The aisles are full of processed foods full of sugars, stabilizers, and dyes.

- Speaking of dye, we've done everything possible to remove it, and it wasn't as hard as I thought. If you look, it's not hard to find dye-free alternatives to most of your favorite things, and there are a couple of grocery stores that make that easier and carry all or mostly dye-free products.

- Make your own bread if you're capable of that kind of thing. I personally am not, but I found friends who make bread, and it's great.

- When my kids make their school lunches, there must be some balance to it. Yes, I let them take a cookie sometimes, but not every day. They can't have a sandwich every day with processed lunch meat, but they can get creative with what they take. We learned a number of interesting school lunch ideas that don't rely on a sandwich every day.

- Make your own lunch meat if you have a sandwich-every-day kind of kid.

- Get chickens if you have the space, time, and the desire.

- Spend time researching products you use every day, like paper towels and toilet paper. This all depends on how crunchy of a person you want to be. I love my crunchy friends who are full sprint into being as kind to nature as possible, but sometimes I just need a paper towel that soaks it all up instantly. Regardless, there are alternatives to most products, especially if they're made with plastic.

- When it comes to physical health, I have learned how to work out all over again, with new boundaries. I'm slowly getting back to lifting. I've always loved lifting weights, and I missed it. It's a slow process and requires a lot of modification for me, but I can do it.

  Saturday mornings are family workouts in the garage with a deck of cards style workout. Again, it's good for everyone for multiple reasons. Great family bonding time.

- Cardio doesn't have to be just running, and I can't run anymore, so I walk/jog. Sometimes I bike, and sometimes I do body weight workouts that keep my heart rate high enough to get some cardio from it, even though that isn't the primary intent

- Do something active. Don't lie around and waste away while life passes you by. Find a recreational sport and learn it. Tennis, golf, pickleball, racquetball, or a walking group. Anything!

Think about it and look through what you have in your cabinets and pantries—all these things are either absorbed into your skin, touch your skin all day, go in your mouth, or on your face (make-up/skin care).

Look at the ingredients. It's important.

This short list of simple changes and additions may be too easy for some. It may also seem overwhelming. Do one at a time if you can't do it all. We were already doing lots of these things before cancer, but not all, and never all at the same time. Now we do all of them all the time. It's just part of life. This is not about surviving; it's about thriving! I didn't live through all that to be unhealthy and unhappy. I'm here to smile and live in joy, feel good, and help others feel good inside and out. I hope to shake up the way people think about everyday things like how we eat, how we shop, what we spend our time on, how we impact our kids, what we teach our kids about themselves, and how we take charge of our overall health.

Simplicity, coupled with thoughtful execution and dedication, can bring immense joy in life. It can bring families together and refocus who you are as a unit.

# 12

## A LETTER TO THE GIRL WHO HAD NO IDEA WHAT WAS COMING: MY YOUNGER SELF

This is a hard concept for me. I've been exposed to and gathered knowledge and life experience, and I've always wondered what I would say to a younger me if I could. In addition to writing this letter to my younger self, I also wrote letters to my daughters. You won't find those in this book, but I recommend it to any parent. Write letters to your kids when they are little, save them, and when they're older, give them the collection. It's easier to do over the years than trying to remember it all at once when they're older. With that said, below is my letter to myself.

Dear young lady,

I have to share some things with you about your life, good and bad. There is no perfect life. Only Jesus accomplished that, and that's a good place to start. You are a young lady with a heart that belongs to the Lord. You have been saved by grace through faith, and the Holy Spirit lives within. Don't allow the world to creep in and separate you and your thoughts from that. Your path will be hard, but pray instead of leaning into the vices of the world. It makes everything easier when you relinquish control and allow the guidance of the Holy Spirit to lead the way. When you stray from a solid footing in your faith, remember that you are a child of God and always will be. Don't stray for too long, and make sure you run back.

Remember where you come from, who you are, and who your family has raised you to be. Your grandparents and parents are so full of knowledge and wisdom, and they have only your best interest at heart, even though it doesn't feel like it at times. They have charted the course that your moral compass will follow. Your moral compass and values are strong. You will have integrity like no other. Sometimes even to a fault. You will be fiercely loyal to those in your small circle, and that will serve you well. Your loyalty and integrity are your code of ethics imprinted in your heart and mind. You'll have times where people betray your trust, and you'll cut them from your life. That's ok. But don't forget to forgive them. Holding onto anger and resentment is like drinking poison. It only hurts you. Those who are supposed to be in your life will admire that code of ethics you have. You have a deep love for people that may feel odd because you won't really like being around people, but you are, at your core, an extrovert. You will be drawn to people, and they will be drawn to you. Please use that for the good of others.

You will be blessed with a husband who isn't anything like you imagined, but he's so much better. Follow your gut feelings and intuition. They are Holy Spirit-led, and he is the ultimate uniter. That gut feeling led you to your husband and will provide a path in your life. Learn your husband well so that you can wholly support him. His career will create what feels like endless difficulties, but will give you a life of excitement, friendship, and bonds in the military that aren't replaceable with anything else. It will be hard, but you will succeed, and your life will feel meaningful just like you wanted. You will always want to leave a place better than you found it, so do that. Don't get so wrapped up in your own mission to do it all that it overshadows your husband. You're an extrovert, a social butterfly, and you're active. He may not always want to be, and that's OK. He will be a homebody who enjoys peaceful evenings, lakes, rivers, mountains, and campfires. You'll fall in love with those.

You're going to be witness to one of the greatest treasures this life can afford you. You're going to have two precious, amazing daughters, and you're going to watch your husband transform into a daddy to them you couldn't have thought possible. It's his thing. He will be involved in everything they do, he will love them unconditionally, and he will show them with his actions what kind of man they should look for in a husband because he will treat you so well and them so well. He will set the standard, and he'll do it with action, not just his words.

Your girls will be the greatest achievement in your life, and watching their personalities bloom will be hugely entertaining. They'll be SO funny, and smart and beautiful and athletic, and they'll love God with all their hearts. You and your husband will need to steer that ship and sometimes it will feel like a pirate ship, but stay the course. Kids don't come to the Lord on their own usually. They need guidance, and they need examples. Y'all will falter and make mistakes. You'll party too much, and you'll cuss too much, and you'll hate that about yourselves. You'll have to ultimately face your vices and kill them in your lives. You can still love a good party, have a drink every now and then, and have your friends. You just can't overindulge. Be open about this process with your kids. Don't hide who you were; that you know you are a Christian living in sin, and the goals about who you are going to become. It's a process, and they should be witness to the transformation. You'll have to painfully move from the attitude of Do as I say, to Do as I do. It will be rewarding for all of you. It's worth it. Don't back down and sink into pity. Just fix the problem. Sanctification is on-going and can be painful, but it's necessary.

By the time you're in your thirties, you will have seen a lot of things living the military lifestyle. You'll have friends everywhere, and your kids will show you their resilience as military kids. You'll be living your best life, and then things will change. I hope you're ready for what your body, mind, heart, and soul will go through because it is going to be excruciating to endure. But you can do it. You were made for such a time as this, and God will be your fourth man in the fire. You're not alone, even when you feel alone.

Cancer will creep in and try to destroy you, but you will overcome. Learn from it, let God use it to change you, and maybe to change others through you. Find a way to fight and win, and when you claim Victory, remember that to God be the Glory.

Victory will be realized after battling through the valleys of darkness and hardship, and it will change the course of your life. You're going to do great things, little lady. Your husband and kids are going to do great things. Don't waste time on things that aren't fruitful. Don't be consumed with work and miss everything your kids are doing. Love them, show up for them, and encourage them. You will be a strict parent cause neither you nor your husband is up for raising nonproductive, unmannered adults who suck the life out of society. Work to balance your rules, your level of strictness, and as your kids grow, alter your approach from dictatorship to democracy in your house. Society will appreciate your kids learning how to be great humans, I promise. Putting in the work and teaching them during their youngest years, when their brains are soaking up knowledge, will pay you back tenfold as they age. As they become preteens, begin giving them more input, ask their opinion on family decisions, and get their thoughts and feelings on situations. Make sure it's appropriate, but work hard to ensure they understand that they are a valued member of your family, and that they matter. You don't have to go with their input, but if you choose not to explain why you're making the decision that you're making. There's value in telling them why. It helps them form their problem-solving thought processes into ones that are extremely productive and will serve them well long term. It will also allow you to teach them that their way may not always be the best way. It may not be wrong, but they'll learn to hear other people, value other people, and work as a team.

Have fun as a family. You never know how much life you're going to get. If you die young, you want your family to have an endless number of memories of you that make them smile because that's all they'll have left. Don't leave them with the memory of you always walking out the door because work, or friends, or events are more important than them.

You're going to live a full, happy, interesting, challenging, and beautiful life. Don't take it for granted. Don't forget that the time to love and serve others is always now and remember that this earth is not your home. You will one day look at the face of Jesus. When it comes to concerns about your own death. You don't need to know; you just need to be ready to go.

You're strong, driven, you're capable of inspiring others, you're loving and caring, you're a do-er, not a talker, and you will apply those skills repeatedly when pouring into others.

Keep your head high, your Bible handy, and your heart ready.

In hope,

*Me*

# ACKNOWLEDGMENTS

For your input, editing, design skills, love, and
encouragement to get this done:

• *Stephanie* •

The multi-tool human behind the execution of many
of my life's shenanigans in all the very best ways.
A+ military spouse and lifetime friend.

• *Jessica* •

Proofreader extraordinaire who allowed me to
keep my wild-west style of writing but fixed all the
commas, a local gal, and lifetime friend.

• *Amanda* •

Giver of many great stories and so many additions
that will help military spouses everywhere, another
A+ military spouse and lifetime friend.

*• Ryan, Candace, and All of My Cancer Fight Club •*

Keep fighting, Heads Held High, and know
that I'm always in your corner.

• My *Discipleship Group* •

For your constant support, love, prayer, and uplifting words:
Jessica (fearless & chaotic group leader), Jacinta (manager of
standards & mental health), Miranda (endless giver of love
& joy), Maya (who always nails the timing in what's needed),
Heather (the calm in the storm & mom to all), and Kearstin
(the practical analyzer who remembers the details)

*• Club Langley •*

Still looking forward to someone winning the lotto so we
can start construction on our recreation of the block and
float into retirement on our lazy river. Love y'all.

*• My Family •*

Mom, Dad, Step-parents, In-laws, and siblings of all kinds.
I love y'all. Parents—ALL of my parents—THANK YOU
for showing up when we needed y'all the most. Thank you
for helping us keep our lives together and always traveling
cross-country to help us, no matter where we live. We love you.

www.ingramcontent.com/pod-product-compliance
Lightning Source LLC
Chambersburg PA
CBHW010939120626
46554CB00008B/2536